1979

The Dilemmas of Corrections

The Dilemmas of Corrections

Rick J. Carlson

with the assistance of
David K. DeWolf
and
Priscilla DeWolf

Lexington Books
D.C. Heath and Company
Lexington, Massachusetts
Toronto   London

Library of Congress Cataloging in Publication Data

Carlson, Rick J.
    The dilemmas of corrections.

    1. Corrections. 2. Punishment. I. DeWolf, David K., joint author. II. De-
Wolf, Priscilla, joint author. III. Title.
HV8665.C27   364.6   75-32223
ISBN 0-669-00346-8

Second printing August 1977.

Published simultaneously in Canada.

Printed in the United States of America.

International Standard Book Number: 0-669-00346-8

Library of Congress Catalog Card Number: 75-32223

Contents

List of Figures

List of Tables

Foreword

Study of the dimensions and causes of crime in the United States and of the social psychological consequences of being a prisoner have traditionally been specialties of academic sociologists. Yet discourses and decisions on public policy in coping with crime have been almost solely the prerogative of lawyers, particularly those who dominate our legislatures. In recent years, however, these two occupations have begun to meet in addressing correctional issues. There has been a spate of publication on prison and parole policy by law professors who take social science findings into account more than was heretofore customary in their profession, and by social scientists who ground themselves in legal thought more than was the wont of their colleagues.

As Rick Carlson says in his introduction, *The Dilemmas of Corrections* is "another try" at accomplishing such a fusion. In my judgment it achieves more than other efforts of this type. Compared to most works by lawyers, it is less glib and sweeping in its assertions on what social science studies demonstrate, and much more aware of the complexities involved in improving knowledge by further research. Compared to most writings by social scientists, it employs more of the language of practical decision-makers and displays cognizance of the multiple interest groups and competing priorities that inevitably affect policy and practice in government.

This book states the issues more comprehensively and with a more up-to-date coverage of evidence and argument than other volumes now available. It does not pontificate with glib generalizations on every problem, but instead, reports the multiple answers available, assesses their validity, and indicates how better answers can be obtained. It leaves the reader aware that there will be different optimum answers for different types of offense and offender. In short, it helps both the concerned citizen and the government policymaker know not just what to think about the dilemmas of dealing with criminals, but *how* to think about them.

Daniel Glaser
University of Southern California

The Dilemmas of
Corrections

Introduction

There are a number of ways to approach the subject of corrections. Most of them yield useful information. For example, studies of the social structure of prison life have taught us about the dynamics of confinement. Similarly, research on penal measures such as imprisonment, probation, and diversion has generated some information about the effectiveness of one measure vis-à-vis another. And recent assessments of the deterrent effects of corrections have given new life to the concept of deterrence. There has also been some recent research focused on other aspects of the criminal justice process, most of which has been facilitated by the Omnibus Crime Control and Safe Streets legislation of 1968. But a nagging problem remains: the crime rate appears to be increasing despite massive expenditures on crime control programs. In addition, the fear of crime has heightened. If this is so, two conclusions can be reached: either the programs have had the wrong focus and, hence, haven't led to crime control, or the variables that influence the incidence of crime are not amenable to amelioration, irrespective of the program.

We can't resolve this dilemma today. First, we simply don't—and may never—know enough about the causes of crime to fashion programs to reduce it. Second, even if we knew more, we might not be willing or able to make the changes necessary to control crime. And third—specifically with respect to corrections—the relationship between correctional interventions and the crime rate is poorly understood, and perhaps far too tenuous to expect corrections to have a significant impact on the incidence of crime. Yet even if this is true, the reality of the crime problem is pressing—it doesn't excuse the failure to try. This book is a "try." Its intent is neither to solve the crisis of crime in the streets nor to identify the causes of crime. Rather, it is an attempt to pose the questions about corrections whose answers would help us understand the relationship between corrections and the crime rate, however limited it may be.

This focus may seem too sharp, in part because there are acknowledged purposes for corrections other than its ostensible impact on the crime rate. But there are at least three reasons for sharpening the task this way. First, a large body of literature already exists on the purposes of corrections—it should be reflected here but not recycled. Second, we are undeniably in a climate of crisis about the criminal justice system; proposals for reform are flying in all directions. Hence, whereas the impact of corrections on crime rates is only one of the purposes of corrections, given this kind of climate, it is essential that we know more about it. Crime may or may not be increasing, but it is rampant; and if corrections has a role, we should know more clearly what it is. Third, whether or not corrections has much impact on the rates of crime, it is still inexorably measured by that impact, whatever it may be.

There is a second focus for the book. Even if we discover that the relationship between corrections and crime is weak, or virtually nonexistent, there would still be a need for a correctional system. It's highly unlikely that the state and federal governments will dismantle their correctional systems just because they can't be shown to influence the incidence or rates of crime appreciably. Corrections does serve other purposes: it provides a vehicle for retribution; it deters; and it can treat those committed to it with justice and fairness. These and other purposes will also be discussed.

There are four premises for the project.

1. We don't know enough about the relationship between corrections and the incidence of crime rates to formulate decisive correctional policy.
2. The opportunity to reshape correctional policy is available because of the lack of guiding principles in correctional theory and practice.
3. Even though the relationship between correctional programs and the crime rate may never be profound, an attempt to demonstrate such relationships is essential.
4. Regardless of the relationship between corrections and crime, corrections serves other purposes—presumably among them is the just and fair treatment of those we choose to punish.

This book is an attempt to "reconceptualize" corrections subject to those premises. Simply put, I will attempt to look at where we have been in corrections, where we are today, and where we seem to be going in terms of both theory and practice. However, to repeat, the purpose is not just a random gallop through the issues. I will give most attention to issues that go directly to the principal focus: what we do and do not know about the relationship between corrections and the incidence of crime.

This book is designed to be general enough to interest most readers. The reasonably well-read citizen should find it useful but there are two real targets. First, the book should serve as a primer for people who are in positions to make decisions about correctional policy and practice. Hypothetically, a state legislator, newly appointed to the committee in the state legislature that has jurisdiction over corrections, is typical of this target audience. Second, and perhaps more important, the book is aimed toward people who are vitally interested in research which might have an influence. Accordingly, I have included a long research agenda in Part IV, where I have tried to identify the critical questions which, if answered, might make a difference.

Background

This book was commissioned by the National Institute of Law Enforcement and Criminal Justice. The project was risky. The idea was to find someone who didn't know too much about corrections and who therefore would be relatively free of preconceived notions. They also wanted to find someone with no allegiances or loyalties either to correctional theories or to constituencies.

I fit the criteria, but because no one is free of bias, and because we lacked knowledge of the field, an advisory group was appointed. The group met and reviewed the manuscript four times. The group was both diverse and knowledgeable. The members were Walter Berns, Professor of Political Science at the University of Toronto; Kenny Jackson, an exoffender and former president of the Fortune Society; William D. Leeke, Commissioner of Corrections for South Carolina; Sir Leon Radzinowicz, University of Cambridge, England; Robert Martinson, Professor of Sociology at City College of New York; Laura Nader, Professor of Legal Anthropology at University of California, Berkeley; Claudewell Thomas, Chairman of the Department of Psychiatry at New Jersey College of Medicine and Dentistry; Billy Wayson, Director of the Correctional Economics Center of the American Bar Association; and Marvin Wolfgang, Director of the Center for Studies in Criminology and Criminal Law at the University of Pennsylvania.[a]

Without overstatement, it is fair to say that the advisory group has been active, interested, and constructively critical; its members have not been shy. But the group has served as a resource, not a "commission." They have helped enormously. For example, it was they who helped narrow the scope of the book, and it was they who insisted on a sharper focus. But, despite their help, they are not responsible for what is said. We—I and my assistants, David K. DeWolf and Priscilla DeWolf—have sought to be objective and balanced, but whether we have succeeded is our responsibility, not the advisory group's.

Organization

The book is divided into five parts. The first two parts create a context for a discussion of corrections today; they are mostly descriptive and serve principally to set up the analysis that follows. Part I defines the book's scope and discusses the limits of corrections. Part II looks to both the past and the present. The past is discussed on the assumption that knowing something about the evolution of penal practice makes it possible to speculate about its future. Parts I and II are mostly descriptive. They compress a substantial amount of theory and research into a few pages. For the corrections expert these parts might be trodden softly, but for the "novice" they will be very helpful if Parts III and IV are to make sense.

Part III is the guts of the book; it is more complex and analytic than Parts I and II, but it is the part that makes or breaks the effort. Parts I and II examine past and present correctional activity, but the future is always only probable.

---

[a]Edward Banfield, Professor of Political Science at the University of Pennsylvania, was also appointed but withdrew prior to completion of the manuscript.

There are "alternative" futures for corrections. It is drifting today, buffeted by many competing objectives. Yet deliberate action might chart a course. Such action requires some hard thinking, based to the extent possible on the results of research. Part III tries to supply some of the thinking. Available research is discussed in general terms, but the emphasis is identifying what we do and do not know about prevailing correctional ideology, practice, and reform movements. Then, finally, we can ask, "Do we want to go there?" Part III is designed for those who might influence that decision.

Part IV is designed for those who will aid in shaping the future of corrections, including both policy-makers and researchers. This part offers a research agenda for the future. It is sparse and to the point. First, a series of pivotal issues is identified (based on the first three parts). Then a longer, less timely list is included. Finally, some issues are discussed that are uniquely amenable to consideration by state criminal justice planning agencies.

Part V is more flavorful and less objective than Part IV—it allows me to add some speculations of my own.

Part I:
The Context for Corrections

1

Where Are We in Corrections?

Perhaps the only way to reduce the crime rate is to reduce the birthrate. Crime seems to have become a permanent fixture in the American landscape—all that seems to be happening is that it is more violent. Yet we still try to control crime. Corrections is only one of the weapons we use, and although it is probably a very limited weapon at best, it has always been the target of reformers. Today it is no different; in fact, reform movements have rarely luxuriated as they do today. Nevertheless, the proposals have led neither to consensus nor to sweeping change. Some reformers believe there are too many people in prisons; others believe there are too few. Some think the failure of corrections to rehabilitate is remediable; others think the system inevitably will fail to reform. Some think the community must be used in corrections; others think the location for corrections should be as far away from the community as possible.

In this turbulent climate, legislators, state governors, correctional officials, and inmate groups are groping for solutions. Yet nothing seems to be happening. Despite the attention and despite the abundance of proposals for reform, the system has been almost impervious to change in recent years. The most barbaric practices of the past have been abandoned, and a few new ideas, such as diversion, have been tried. But to a large degree, proposals for reform are stacked up outside the prison walls. Some of the reasons for this are discussed as we go along, but the question is raised again in Part III.

The "Topography" of Corrections

Inmate no. 1769 is young and black because, disproportionately, such is the case. His four-foot-by-eight-foot cell is in a prison located about 300 miles from nowhere. He's been there a little over two years for assault with a deadly weapon, growing out of an altercation in a park. He's due for parole in about six months and probably won't make it because he's accumulated a few infractions. He's a member of the prison Afro-American Association; he plays on the softball team and is trying to learn how to paint. He is fairly diligent and has high hopes for a job when he gets out; he helps to operate a vintage lathe in the prison shop. When he gets out in a few years he will be 26 and unmarried; he'll have about $50 and bus fare home.

Inmate no. 1769 is one of approximately 200,000 inmates in custody today.[1] In addition, 140,000 people are in jails, either awaiting trial or serving short-term commitments.[2] They are kept, along with Inmate no. 1769, in 325 state-maintained institutions and 25 penitentiaries in the federal system. There are 96.4 prisoners per 100,000 population.[3]

It costs the Federal Bureau of Prisons about $150 million to do business;[4] in 1937 it cost only $11.5 million. An estimate of the total system cost of state and federal systems combined is $2.7 billion;[5] the system employs 190,000 people.[6] In addition to those put in prisons, about 800,000 are on parole or probation.[7] An undetermined additional number are participating in special correctional programs such as diversion.

This is the simple topography of corrections. There is more to it. Where are we today in terms of programs and practices? In fall 1973, I chaired a working group at the Western American Assembly meetings on the theme "Prisoners in America."[8] The group was diverse: it sought to accommodate the views of three or four correctional heads from western states, three exconvicts, and three or four prison reform activists. In between, spatially as well as philosophically, was an odd collection of "moderates," including well-intentioned citizens, a few students, a Quaker, and a few liberal lawyers. Near the end of the workshop when the issues began to crystallize, the following exchange occurred between an excon, the president of the Prisoners' Union, and a lawyer who had been president of the San Francisco Bar Association:

Excon. What we want is punishment.
Lawyer. What did you say? Did you say that prisoners want to be punished?
Excon. Yes, we want to end the mind-f—— and the indeterminate sentence; we want to be punished the same for each crime that we get caught for.
Lawyer. You mean that you don't want treatment; you don't want to be helped—you just want to serve your time?
Excon. Yes.
Lawyer. I don't believe it.

The past and future are both here—we are in transition between them. We are not yet in a "new" era of corrections. We are leaving certain ideas behind us and are formulating new ones. We have become convinced that rehabilitation cannot live up to its rave notices. We also know that social and environmental conditions are inextricably related to crime, but we don't know how. Many of us, more every day, have come to believe that the fortress prison must be eliminated although we know it will take time. Moreover, many of us agree that, irrespective of the setting, we imprison too many for too long. And many of us also will concede that very little of what we do under the banner of corrections, incarceration or otherwise, works—in the sense that we can't seem to reduce recidivism. And we know that inhumanities always seem to spring from promising reforms. In fact, we have become suspicious of innovation. At most, we are in a period of humanizing consolidation.

We also are beginning to work with some emergent ideas. We know, although we can't be precise, that a small but irreducible number of offenders probably must be incarcerated. Some also believe that some rehabilitation programs will work if we could create noncoercive settings for their implementation, and even some still think they will work with or without coercion. Although criminology too infrequently has been focused on the real concerns of corrections, we are beginning to learn that contributions can be made: econometric analysis and analysis focused on sociodemographic variables such as age are a few. And we have begun to explore the community and its resources as a promised setting in which to create correctional programs, although we haven't provided a coherent framework for their implementation. We also have acknowledged the need to introduce more legal protections for inmates, as we have begun to chop away at the most obvious sources of unfettered discretion. Some of us are also serious about reducing both the number and duration of institutional commitments, recognizing that there is evidence that we may have been too punitive. Finally, we have begun to reintroduce deterrence and retribution to the debate, recognizing that punishment should more closely approximate the gravity of the offense and be less geared to the peculiar and presumed needs of the offender. But in the final analysis we are cautious because we have learned that reform can be reactionary.

Is Change Possible?

Is a sudden transformation of correctional practice possible? I have said that corrections is in transition, moving away from past goals toward some new, but hazily articulated, objectives. This transition may be thought of as a "paradigm shift," although the phrase has been overworked. Nevertheless, are we at the point of a paradigm shift in corrections—a movement through uncertainty towards a different and clearer understanding of the purposes of correction?

Thomas Kuhn offers a simple schematic, which has been embellished by other thinkers, in order to assess whether we are in "transition."[9] His original analysis concerned the nature of paradigm shifts in scientific thought, but it can be applied here. There are essentially four steps.[a] The first is the accumulation of bits of data that don't "fit." At first this information is either ignored or discounted, but as the bits increase, they become more difficult to ignore or argue away. At the second stage, because of accumulating information, the old explanations begin to make less sense—serious "cracks" in the accepted explanation become visible. At about this time new ideas—new explanations—also begin to appear. In this third, transitional stage, there is not yet any consolidation, but new explanations begin to compete with old ones. Finally, at the fourth step, consensus snaps into view, sometimes suddenly. A new and different way of looking at things emerges, which supplies the explanation for both the new data and the new ideas.

---

[a]This four-step scheme varies somewhat from Kuhn's theory; it is a combination of his ideas and those of other thinkers.

In the history of ideas, the Industrial Revolution, the Renaissance, and the Reformation are among the most fundamental paradigm shifts. These movements encompassed broad transformations in cultural perspective. And although it is unlikely that major shifts in perspective occur in subsystems without a preceding transformation in the larger order, some changes in subsystems can occur nevertheless. Examples include the rise of the multinational corporation, changes in musical composition and taste—or closer to home, a dramatic increase in the use of plea bargaining. Medicine is also a good example: a highly technical, sophisticated and specialized medicine is beginning to yield to a more humanistic, less technology-intensive medicine.

How do these boundary conditions for change fit corrections today? First, information that has undermined the rehabilitation model has been accumulating steadily. Enough inconsistent information now exists so that it cannot be—and is not being—ignored. Moreover, some new ideas—a return to retribution, the reconsideration of punishment and deterrence, and community-based correctional programs—have surfaced. These ideas are now competing with older perspectives for allegiance. Hence we may be at the third or transitional state of change. This proposition is also supported by the absence of a new integrating or synthesizing concept. In other words, although we may be at a transition point, no critical mass of support has developed for a new, embracing theory.

There is one major limitation to this analysis. A paradigm shift must move on new ideas or at least freshly conceptualized ones, not the revivification of old ones. Most of the ideas in corrections are simply differently attired old ideas. Therefore a fundamental change in corrections can't be confidently predicted unless a new view of the nature of humanity itself emerges. Change does seem to be taking place, but whether a wholly new way of looking at the question will emerge is problematic. The corrections of the future may simply be one of the "corrections" of the past.

The Central Issues

Despite the resistance of the correctional system, the times may nevertheless be ripe for change. Few are satisfied with things as they are. The public's attention is more riveted on corrections than usual because of the publicity attending recent prison riots—and even more pointedly, the imprisonment of major public figures such as Jimmy Hoffa, Judge Otto Kerner, and many of the key Watergate figures. Unfortunately, no clear vision of the future has emerged. We don't have clear answers about what the prison's role or size or location should be. We don't know enough about the deterrent and incapacitative effects of corrections, although we have a lot of evidence that the system has failed to rehabilitate. Moreover, we don't know nearly enough about who commits what crimes, how often, and why. Finally, we simply aren't clear about whom to "correct," in what way, for how long, where, and why.

Because we lack definitive, reliable answers for these basic questions, policy-makers are constantly torn by conflicting advice: build more prisons versus don't build any; reduce overcrowding in facilities versus incarcerate more for longer; rehabilitate versus punish for only a fixed term; shift corrections to the community versus keep it (and "them") where they are; and so on. And the pressures for some sort of change are mounting. Inmates are increasingly restive, and supervisory personnel are chafing at new restrictions and regulations. There are even occasional strikes and walkouts. But the greatest single source of pressure is political. In a climate of fear, crime control is a very potent political issue. And given the data, as poor and unreliable as they are, the criminal justice system is not doing the job the public expects it to do. The correctional system receives its share of the heat even though its role in crime containment is relatively small. As a result, action will be taken because failure to do something is seen as poor politics. The initiatives that will be taken will affect the correctional system even though few are clear about what to do.

In this atmosphere, salient questions are better than stupid or unintelligible answers. The largest issue is crime itself. Obviously, the rates and incidence of crime and, more specifically, the various types of crime should be known. How much is there, is it increasing in general, and what about violent crime?

This inquiry also must raise questions about the distribution of crime throughout the population, by type of crime and by type of offender. Similarly, recidivism rates (for selected offender categories) both in terms of rearrest and reincarceration are fundamental.

The "dangerous" (and/or "habitual") offender is also high on the list—who or what is a dangerous and/or habitual offender, and what special disposition, if any, should be made of such offenders?

The large cluster of variables that influence the rates and incidence of crime also must be identified, with attention to the impact that corrections might have on those variables. The variables obviously include a host of social, economic, and environmental factors. I will not undertake a detailed examination of the causes of crime because the subject is far too large and because many criminologists argue that it is a fruitless pursuit due to our inability to demonstrate causal relationships. Nonetheless, the relationships between corrections and the other major variables associated with crime must be identified if corrections is to be deployed as a strategic weapon in society's attempts to reduce crime.

Many reform proposals are pending in the criminal justice and corrections system today. Many have a direct bearing on correctional practice. For example, an innovation such as the diversion of selected (and presumed) offenders out of the traditional criminal justice process has an inevitable impact on corrections.

Most students of criminology and corrections recognize the relativity of both the definitions of crime and the tools used to treat the criminal. What was common practice a century ago may seem savage today; the use of the stocks is an example. Hence any attempt to look at corrections as a dynamic, evolutionary system must reflect the historical fact of relativity.

Relativity also characterizes the philosophies of crime and its control and the philosophies of punishment. There have been many schools of criminology, and many theories of punishment. Today we are rudderless; we have lost certainty about the value and validity of the theories that corrections was premised on. Some theories have been repudiated, perhaps only temporarily; still others, which were abandoned in the past, now show signs of life. So we remain in flux. Nevertheless, because correctional practice reflects its theoretical buttressing, any examination of corrections today, particularly a reconceptualization, must determine the role of the philosophies of criminal behavior in correctional practice.

However relative the theory, and however varied the instruments of punishment, punishment remains a brute social fact. We have chosen to call it by many different names—retribution, rehabilitation, and so forth—but it has always underpinned our correctional methods, even if it was unarticulated. Given the presence of punishment, there are a number of salient issues about the setting and location for punishment: What is the appropriate size of the penal institution, or the probation or parole caseload? Where should correctional programs be situated? Where should prisons be built? Which communities are ripe for correctional experimentation? And so forth.

If the focus of corrections is the "offense"—which has seldom been the case in recent years—other questions arise. The first question, again, is relativity. An offense to the industrialized United States would not necessarily have been a threat to our rustic agrarian past—a horsethief was a greater villain when horses were the sole means of conveyance. Criminal law has gradually been retooled to apply to behavior that is least tolerable at any time. This phenomenon raises two hot contemporary issues: the decriminalization of certain acts—often called victimless crimes—and the relationship between the penalty and the offense, if the offense stays on the books.

A related set of issues can be classified under the rubric "rights of the accused"—that is, law developed to ensure that alleged offenders are treated fairly in the course of their prosecution. Another set of questions includes sentencing, judicial discretion, and the indeterminacy of sentences.

The offense may be important, but most of the attention in contemporary criminology and corrections has been lavished on the offender. Considering this dimension engenders a host of critical questions, including:

1. What do we know about offenders, sociodemographically or otherwise?
2. What evidence about the offender has been marshalled by the various disciplines—including biology, economics, behavioral science, law, and sociology—and what are the consistencies and inconsistencies in these perspectives?
3. What about the dangerous offender? Can he or she be identified? If so, what are the implications for correctional practice?

4. What "contribution" does the known offender make to the overall crime rate, as to types of offenders and types of offenses?
5. What treatment modalities, if any, have "worked," and with what type of offender?
6. What are the recidivism rates of various types of offenders?
7. What are the views, attitudes, and beliefs of offenders?
8. Does crime pay for some offenders? If so, for which offenders, and to what degree?

Whatever the definition of an offense, and whoever the offender turns out to be, there will always be a "means" of corrections. The issues here include the type and impact of various correctional programs; the degree to which coercion is exercised to compel participation; and the relationships among the major correctional modalities, such as incarceration, probation, parole, and diversion.

It is also in this context that the "economy" of corrections will be explored. How much of correctional practice is impervious to change because it is conducted for reasons essentially unrelated to the reform of offenders, except insofar as offenders supply the necessary raw material?

A final major category of issues is "community-based corrections." Whereas it is properly a question of the location of corrections, it has become both the tag-word and catchall for a great many related correctional reforms. The central issues here include the scale and breadth of innovation; its relationship to probation and other conventional community-based correctional programs; its relative efficacy as a correctional modality vis-à-vis conventional practices; the relative degree of coerciveness exercised; and the use of surveillance to ensure security as a substitute for confinement.

I have not mentioned all the issues, but I have mentioned those that represent the major themes. Most of them will have to be resolved one way or another in the next few years. Unfortunately, there are few clear guidelines because we simply don't know very much.

Notes

1. *Prisoners in State and Federal Institutions on December 31, 1971, 1972, and 1973* (Washington, D.C.: Government Printing Office, 1975), p. 1.

2. *Survey of Inmates of Local Jails, 1972* (Washington, D.C.: U.S. Department of Justice, n.d.), p. 1.

3. *Prisoners in State and Federal Institutions*, p. 18.

4. *Expenditure and Employment Data for the Criminal Justice System, 1972-73* (Washington, D.C.: Government Printing Office, 1975), p. 17.

5. Ibid., p. 17.

6. Ibid., p. 43.

7. See Ronald Goldfarb and Linda Singer, *After Conviction* (New York: Simon and Schuster, 1973), p. 14.

8. See "Challenging Criminal Corrections" (Berkeley, Calif.: The Institute for Local Self-government, 1973).

9. Thomas Kuhn, *The Structure of Scientific Revolutions* (Chicago: University of Chicago Press, 1962).

2 The Limits of Corrections

On a given day most if not all the laws are broken. And on a given day many different people engage in lawbreaking: speeders, drinkers, assaulters, embezzlers, price-fixers, and even little kids ripping off baseball cards. Out of all this activity, only a few actors are apprehended. Many offenses are systematically ignored: gambling in the affluent suburbs, erratic driving by elected officials, corporate boardroom conspiracies, public assaults that bystanders ignore, and thefts by employees. Sometimes no one sees or hears what happens, or sometimes the crime is discovered later. Many crimes aren't reported even if someone knows of their occurrence: historically, women have failed to report rapes, and both men and women have failed to report assaults that threaten their pride. Small thefts are often better absorbed than reported because insurance rates would surely go up. And husbands and wives tolerate mutual assaults rather than publicize their problems.

But of the crimes that are reported, only a few are ever solved—or "cleared," to use the technical term. When the perpetrator isn't known—as is most often the case—only 12 percent of serious crime is cleared.

Then there is police discretion. Probably more unchecked discretion is exercised by police than anywhere else in the discretion-riddled criminal justice system. Police make myriad choices in their work: whether to pursue or not, whether to arrest or not, and so on. And although the police reflect many of the values of the larger society in their choices, they also execute a rough justice of their own. But at least at the point of actual apprehension, we have an identifiable pool of potential inmates—or do we?

First there is "diversion." Although not uniformly, in some jurisdictions potential inmates are diverted out of the criminal justice system into special programs that afford the participant a relatively rich package of support services.[a] This diversion, of course, is a form of corrections. And unless the participant runs amuck, he or she will never end up in a cell.

Next there is the question of charges. Arrest isn't synonymous with formal charges—the arrest has to stick, and if the prosecutor's office can't make it stick, the alleged offender must be flushed out of the system. Approximately 70 to 80 percent of the cases sent to the prosecutor by the police are never prosecuted (see Figure 2-2). In addition, the prosecutor may discharge some of those arrested for other reasons—politics or graft may figure in. In some cases crime control strategy may dictate release because the release of some offenders may lead to their bosses.

---

[a]This subject will be discussed in greater detail in Chapter 5.

Finally, we have the dialectics of lawyers and judges. In the tug and pull of plea-bargaining and the rest of the pretrial rituals, discretion is freely scattered. Prosecutors may be convinced to reduce the charges or to eliminate one or more charges (having pressed too many originally, their "mercy" translates into tactics). Judges, facing heavy caseloads, may willingly go along with bargains that eliminate the need for a trial; often they may "force" it. And defense lawyers, whose fees are secured without trials, will push hard for a deal. The defendants, the only ones with a real stake in the outcome, don't have much to say—the deals are forced on them.

Thus throughout the drama the number of potential inmates steadily diminishes. Let's assume that a few get through—for whatever reason they have run the gauntlet and are still eligible for prison. They have been tried and found guilty, or they have accepted a plea bargain that holds the possibility of imprisonment. They still have a chance; judges inevitably order a presentence investigation to aid them in deciding what to do. Once again the opportunity arises to deprive the offender of his cell. Eventually sentence is imposed on the remaining offenders. And once it is, the pool of offenders is relatively fixed. Discretion is exercised again in the prison, principally in the parole process; but if a sentence of incarceration has been imposed, escape routes are cut off.

Edward Banfield, in his book *The Unheavenly City Revisited,*[1] includes a chart (reprinted as Figure 2-1) that shows graphically the "shrinkage" in the pool of potential inmates. Another chart (reprinted as Figure 2-2) from *Crime and Justice: American Style*, by Clarence Schrag,[2] reflects the same phenomenon by depicting the impact of discretion from the point of arrest to final disposition.[b]

There are two points to be raised here. First, corrections doesn't make any choices about what it gets. Once the inmate is there, it can try to influence him or her; but unlike other processors of products, it can't select its own raw material. In this sense the comment that prisons can't be improved until they get a better class of prisoners may be perversely accurate.

Second, the data raise a central question in this inquiry: What is the relationship between corrections and the incidence of crime? Corrections is synonymous with crime in the minds of many, in part because of the rehabilitative thrust in contemporary corrections. When crime rates soar, as they often appear to, anger is frequently directed at the correctional system: "Why are those crooks coddled? Why can't we throw the key away? Why aren't those guys rehabilitated?" It's like the 55-year-old patient faulting the medical profession for her lung cancer after forty years of heavy smoking. Yet there must be some relationship between corrections and the crime rate. The main question is, what is its nature and extent?

---

[b]Figures 2-1 and 2-2 tend to exaggerate the amount of crime actually "unpunished" because many of those in the final "circle" of those imprisoned are responsible for a substantial portion of crimes that are unreported, unprosecuted, and so forth. The figures thus illustrate the process of selection; they are not strictly accurate.

Total Serious Crimes[a] U.S. 1968: 9,000,000

Based on Estimates

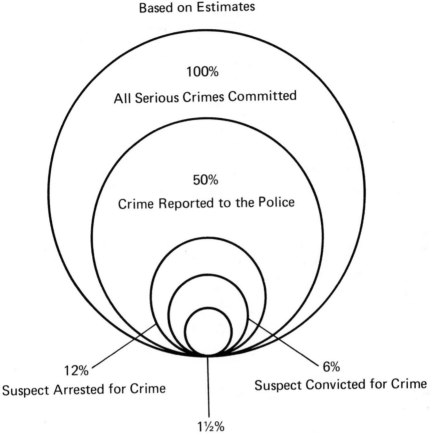

100%

All Serious Crimes Committed

50%

Crime Reported to the Police

12%

Suspect Arrested for Crime

6%

Suspect Convicted for Crime

1½%

Suspect Imprisoned for Crime

[a]Aggregate of homicide, forcible rape, robbery, aggravated assault, burglary, larceny over $50, auto theft.

Source: Edward C. Banfield, *The Unheavenly City Revisited* (Boston: Little, Brown, 1974), p. 202. Data taken from *Final Report* of the National Commission on the Causes and Prevention of Violence (Washington, D.C.: Government Printing Office, 1969), p. xviii.

Figure 2-1. Crime and Law Enforcement.

There are some other questions. Does corrections deal with only some offenders? How many offenses are never prosecuted, much less detected, because of the operation of myriad selection factors, many of which are culturally determined? Do those who end up in prison represent only a small, but as yet undefinable, percentage of those who commit crimes? Are people who

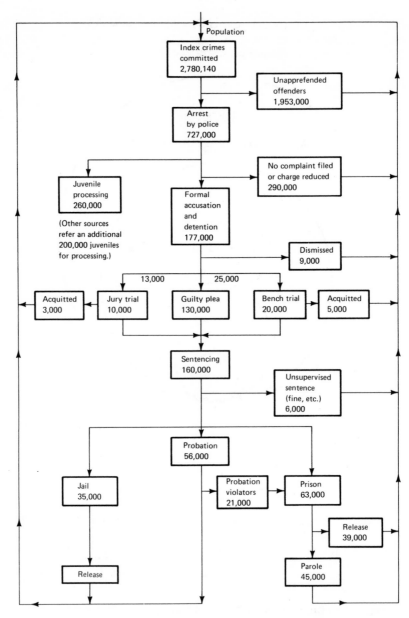

Source: Clarence Schrag, *Crime and Justice: American Style* (Washington, D.C.: Government Printing Office Publication no. HSM 72-9052, 1971), p. 3. Adapted from the President's Commission on Law Enforcement and Administration of Justice, *The Challenge of Crime in a Free Society* (Washington, D.C.: Government Printing Office, 1967), pp. 262-263.

Figure 2-2. Criminal Justice System Model (with estimates of flow of offenders for Index Crimes in the United States in 1965).

don't get into cells the people who commit the bulk of the crimes? It is frequently argued that those who are released from incarceration account for a disproportionate (and perhaps grossly disproportionate) amount of the total crime. Unfortunately, we don't have the answers to these puzzles. It may be that corrections ends up with those who do the worst deeds, and it may even be true that corrections briefly incapacitates those capable of the worst depredation. But even if this is so, given the volume of crime, corrections might still have little control over the overall crime rate. Those who end up in cells may have committed only a small portion of all the crimes. If they were all released tomorrow, would the effect on the crime rate be that noticeable?

The real question here is resource allocation: What is the appropriate "profile" for corrections? If crime control is the only measure of the criminal justice system, with recidivism rates what they apparently are, corrections might have a hard time justifying its share of the criminal justice dollar. On the other hand, if the deterrent, incapacitative, and retributive purposes of corrections were more clearly understood, a larger slice of the dollar pie might be claimed. Finally, it is important that corrections remember the cause of justice—whether or not it "cures," it can still treat offenders humanely.

Notes

1. Edward C. Banfield, *The Unheavenly City Revisited* (Boston: Little, Brown, 1974).

2. Clarence Schrag, *Crime and Justice: American Style* (Washington, D.C.: Government Printing Office, Publication no. HSM 72-9052, 1971).

Part II:
Where We've Been and
Where We're Going

3

The Permanence of Punishment: The Eras of Corrections

Look at today's prison or yesterday's prison—it doesn't make much difference; they're usually the same. Twenty-five prisons in the United States are over 100 years old. Sixty-one prisons that opened at the turn of the century are still in business.[1]

Asylums shown in lithographs from our antebellum past don't look very different from today's prison.[2] There are new prisons around, and there is a new prison architecture,[3] but the prison most of us see in our minds, the decaying relic, is still the prison that Inmate no. 1769 occupies.

It is common to ascribe an array of purposes to corrections: to isolate, to protect the community, to allow for penitence, to gain retribution—"just deserts"—and most recently, to treat and rehabilitate. But rarely is the barebones argument made that the purpose of corrections is to punish. Fundamentally, however, that is what is done, regardless of what else may be done as well. As Herbert Packer puts it, "Not all punishment is criminal punishment, but all criminal punishment is punishment."[4] The means and methods have changed, almost as much as the rhetoric, but corrections has punished and continues to do so. What philosophy is punishment based on, and what are the implications of that base for the nature of the punishment imposed?

All the major articulated purposes of corrections—social defense, incapacitation, retribution, deterrence, and rehabilitation—are incorporated into correctional experience. All these purposes are irreducibly philosophies of punishment. But while that is true, it is also true that the proffered purposes of punishment have changed over time. Hence this chapter has two objectives: first, to lay out the ingredients of corrections that have been combined and recombined in various recipes, in varying proportions; and second, based on these ingredients, to delineate the "eras" of corrections that have led to the present.

The Varieties of Punishment

Imprisonment is only one way to punish. Historically, the prison is a recent invention in the Western world. The Greeks had no use for it, and throughout most of the middle ages other means of punishment were practiced—including mutilation, torture, exile, degradation, and fines and reparations. Banishment was another method: a large portion of Australia was settled by exiles from

23

England; almost 140,000 persons were given one-way tickets.[5] And when Australia wasn't the destination, it was the colonies here. The prison as a "house of correction" didn't emerge until the mid-sixteenth century in England.[6] And it wasn't until the late eighteenth and early nineteenth centuries that the prison as we conceive it today was constructed. Nevertheless the prison is still our least-used weapon.[a] Edwin Sutherland and Donald Cressey show, for example, that "In the United States . . . the imposition of a fine is by far the most frequent method of reacting punitively to crime; probably more than 75 percent of penalties imposed are fines."[7]

The prison is still viewed by most as a place of last resort. Some, like John Bartlow Martin in *Break Down the Walls*, have argued for decarceration:

The American prison system makes no sense. Prisons have failed as deterrents to crime. They have failed as rehabilitative institutions. What then shall we do? Let us face it: Prisons should be abolished. The prison cannot be reformed. It rests upon false premises. Nothing can improve it. It will never be anything but a graveyard of good intentions. Prison is not just the enemy of the prisoners. It is the enemy of society. This behemoth, this monster error, has nullified every good work. It must be done away with.[8]

This opinion is even shared by a few, like William Nagel, who because of their experience in corrections might not be expected to be so rash.[b] Others, more cautious by nature, argue that every alternative should be explored before the prison is used. Norval Morris and Gordon Hawkins include this ukase in *The Honest Politician's Guide to Crime Control:* "Unless cause to the contrary can be shown, the treatment of offenders shall be community-based."[9]

The prison may be a modern correctional instrument, but it remains the cornerstone of penology because it looms as a backstop: to the offender it represents the worst that can be done, short of execution. In other words, the prison may be essential if corrections is to have a shed of punitive tools that are graded in severity. Yet it is only one of the tools available; probation, parole, and a few other methods can be used also. Facing a swarm of objections to incarceration, some judges have fashioned some imaginative penalties. Some prefer sending the offenders back to the street instead of incarcerating them. But still the range of options is sparse: the fine, perhaps restitution, probation, or prison. And for a special few, diversion programs are available. But that's about it.

---

[a]The exception is for crimes weighted in severity.

[b]Nagel isn't unequivocal, but in "With Friends Like These, Who Needs Enemies?" he argues, "In my relatively inconspicuous way, I've been telling people . . . that prisons are inherently evil. I was not speaking or writing, however, of those built decades ago. I was referring to 103 of the newest so-called correctional facilities in America, all of which I visited during 1971 and early 1972." *Crime and Delinquency* 20 (July 1974):226.

The Varieties of Purpose

Many purposes have been ascribed to punishment. Chief among them are retribution, social defense, deterrence and rehabilitation.

Retribution

Sutherland and Cressey argue that "Criminal procedure is to resentment what marriage is to affection: namely the legal provision for the inevitable impulse of human beings."[10] The root idea is revenge. Somehow a wound has been inflicted on the corporate body, and in a kind of homeostatic way a wound must be inflicted on the wrongdoer. Justice demands revenge. Society's failure to punish the offender would inevitably diminish social values.[c]

In strict terms there are two major variations in retributive theory: revenge and expiation. The first looks to society's motive, even right, to punish. The second looks to the offender's possible gain as well: punishment having been inflicted, the offender has an opportunity to expiate his or her guilt and resume an acceptable position in society.

It is easy to treat this position too simplistically. It can indeed be simply stated, but it involves some complex considerations. Revenge no doubt accompanies the administration of justice; if it didn't, humanizing the correctional experience wouldn't be so difficult. There is also an "automaticism" about it: if an offense is committed, it is assumed that punishment should follow; whether it should be in proportion to the offense is at least debatable. Then there is the symbolic dimension. This is more than deterrence because there is the assumption that even if the correctional system utterly failed to deter, punishment still would be required because it fits some sort of cultural urging for proportion—a kind of "natural justice" seems to compel it.

Today, few cling to the bald premise of retribution—that any offense necessitates inflicting pain. To use Nigel Walker's terms, most espouse "compromising" or "limiting" retributivism.[11] They find room for other considerations, including humanism and deterrence. These compromises stem from a distaste for the "primitive" nature of the pure retributive formula. This distinction has led to a number of alternative formulations that introduce those "other considerations." They include proportionality to the offense as a limit to severity, the need for a link between the offense and society's moral sensitivity, and so on. These considerations have contaminated the pure retributive formula, yet ultimately, the erosion of the retributivist position is limited by politics. According to Walker, "The strongest case for [a] sophisticated form of

---

[c]Essentially, this was Kant's position.

retributivism is not that to breach it occasionally is unthinkable or morally unsupportable, but that to abandon it completely is politically out of the question."[12]

In part, these political realities led the Committee for the Study of Incarceration to revive the principle of retribution in a forthcoming report.[13] The committee, directed by Andrew Von Hirsch, developed a new model for corrections, which is fundamentally based on the notion of just deserts. The committee draft recognizes the "man-in-the-street" basis for retribution but develops a more sophisticated system of punishment. The report, like many other expressions in corrections recently, springs from a rejection of the rehabilitative ideal. It reflects the impoverishment of rehabilitation by arguing that the penalty must fit the crime, not the criminal. To do so, an elaborate scheme of social weights and measures has to be constructed. Through means not fully developed, society must somehow be given the opportunity to vote on the nature, duration, and severity of penalties. Thus the committee's position, although it is retributive, reflects the need to assess both the content and methods of contemporary punishment.

The idea of retribution is regaining strength. If the offender cannot be reformed, and if the threat to society from the premature release or lenient treatment of the offender is too great, what is left? Society must have some justification for the price it exacts from the offender, even if it is only symbolic. Most simply stated, the justification is that the offense warrants a response calibrated with its severity. The attractiveness of the retributive formula then is threefold: first, it is simple and unadorned; second, it resonates with some deep-seated impulse in society to match bad with bad and good with good; and third, it relieves society of the responsibility of making other purposes, such as rehabilitation and/or deterrence, "work."

Social Defense

Social defense is the most straightforward of the justifications for punishment. Criminal acts harm society, and thus to protect it, criminal activity must be "neutralized." The means should be those most calculated to protect—whether simple incapacitation or treatment. To this point, concepts of social defense are compatible with most other theories of punishment. But there are some incompatibilities.

Most proponents of this perspective look almost exclusively to society and its protection, not to the offender.[d] This doesn't mean that the advocate of social defense is necessarily opposed to any due process protections for the offender.

[d]There are exceptions, such as Marc Ancel, *Social Defence: A Modern Approach to Criminal Problems* (New York: Schocken, 1966). Ancel argues that an accommodation can be made between "social needs" for protection and the "cure" of the individual.

But what is done to the offender is of much less concern than that something is done and that that something removes the threat. Incarceration is obviously effective for the individual stuck in the cell, but then so is the death penalty. The idea of punishment itself is unnecessary; the primary objective is neutralization: The threat must be removed or rendered ineffective. Society may punish, then, but not because the offender in some sense deserves punishment or because society has an abstract right to punish. Punishment can be defended only as a means to an end: defense of the community. Of course, this can be accomplished in two principal ways: systematic elimination of the threat, or rigorous prevention measures designed to blunt it. Both ways are pursued, but the theory also explains the development of sophisticated crime prevention measures.[14] Given the seeming intractability of the crime problem, prophylaxis has become necessary.

Social defense theorists are interested in the individual, however, in one quite specific way. To the extent to which antisocial behavior can be predicted, the efficiency of social defense can be enhanced, because if potential offenders can be identified, their detention can be justified by the community's need for safety. In this sense, then, the "social defense" advocate is also a positivist. To quote Jerome Hall: "The Positive School is committed to the thesis that any measure necessary to protect society (the accused, and, of course, the convicted person are automatically excluded therefrom) is justifiable."[15] As a result, theorists in the school aren't particularly charmed with notions of due process, or for that matter, with much of the criminal law.[16] Hence it is the "social defender" who wishes to ferret out the dangerous offender for special attention. The preventive detention legislation recently enacted in the District of Columbia owes its gestation to this philosophy. But "dangerousness" is a very fuzzy concept.[e] Predictions are made continuously; the standard presentence investigation and most probation and parole decisions are based, at least in part, on predictions about future behavior. But there is a difference. However faulty these latter predictions may be, at least the question of guilt has already been resolved in a setting in which the alleged offender has benefited from an array of protections designed to force the truth down a narrow tunnel. In social defense theory, however, the question of guilt is far less important than the question of proclivity (in part because punishment need not be carefully calibrated with the gravity of the offense). Packer looks at it this way:

Incapacitation has a much subtler and more attenuated relationship to the nature of the offense. To the extent that there is any connection at all, it rests on a prediction that a person who commits a certain kind of crime is likely to commit either more crimes of the same sort or other crimes of other sorts.[17]

But again, this presupposes some skill in prediction, unless we are willing to tolerate a large number of "false positives"—those deemed dangerous who are

---

[e]This subject is addressed at length in Chapter 5.

not. It may be acceptable to perform ten biopsies for every one pathology, but if the result is imprisonment as opposed to the loss of a slice of tissue, that ratio may not be acceptable. And this would probably be true, given our current sense of social ethics, even if predictive methods were more reliable, which they aren't.[18] Morris and Hawkins, after examining the evidence, conclude that "Control over another man's life is too serious a matter to be posited on other than tested, evaluated, refined experience—on carefully validated prediction tables."[19],f Some argue that the matter is too serious to consider at all.

Social defense lives a resilient life. Recent alarums sounded by former Attorney General William Saxbe, among others, about the "habitual" criminal owe their origins to it.[g] The common-sense roots of the idea are understandable—society should protect itself. The trouble begins with the branches—the logical extensions of the theory. For example, without mitigating circumstances, the most effective punishment would be decapitation.[h] It's simple, cheap, highly effective, and incapacitative, at least to the decapitee. Or all offenders could be given life terms. But once these measures are rejected, the social defense theorist must accept mitigating circumstances, presumably arising out of justice and fairness. Some crimes are less heinous and hense less objectionable; still other individuals who commit certain crimes may have done so for reasons that may serve to soften the state's otherwise harsh response, and so on. As long as mitigating circumstances are considered, social defense must serve as only one parameter of retribution.

Deterrence

Newsweek recently quoted California Governor Edmund G. Brown, Jr., as saying, "We face a real problem with prisons. They don't rehabilitate, they don't deter, they don't punish, and they don't protect."[20] Even allowing for political fudging, the governor is wrong. Prisons do all these things, except perhaps to rehabilitate. They do punish, and they do protect—at least while they incapacitate—and they do deter. But how much does the prison deter? Franklin Zimring has written:

No matter how complex one's theory of human motivation, it is plausible to suppose that attaching the threat of unpleasant consequences to behavior will

---

fThere may, however, be a distinction between predictions about persons who have never committed an offense and those who are exoffenders. I return to this point in Chapter 5.

gLEAA has recently awarded $3 million for a study of "career criminals." See *American Journal of Correction* (January-February 1975):33.

hGeorge Bernard Shaw had no hesitation in recommending execution. In *The Crime of Imprisonment* (New York: Citadel Press, 1946), he wrote, "The attempt to reform an incurably dangerous criminal may come to be classed with the attempt to propitiate a sacred rattlesnake. The higher civilization does not make still greater sacrifices to the snake: it kills it" (p. 64).

reduce the tendency of people to engage in that behavior. And stated this simply, the hypothesis that criminal punishments tend to be deterrent is quite similar to the theories that underlie our national defense strategies, behaviorist psychology, and the way in which costs influence decisions in the marketplace. In this general frame of reference, the theory that threatened punishment serves as a mechanism to reduce crime among potential offenders is unimpeachable.[21]

Much of this seems to be common sense. Johannes Andenaes suggests that as long as research results aren't available, policy-makers and judges must base their decisions on common sense. To Andenaes, this means that the focus should be to what degree, and under which conditions, it is possible to control behavior by the threat of punishment.[22]

In discussing deterrence, at least two critical distinctions should be made: the differences between absolute and marginal deterrence, and that between general and specific deterrence. The first distinction is relatively clear: The death penalty is an absolute deterrent, as might be impalement for the chicken thief. But for the bulk of crimes, the germane question is, "What penalties will produce the greatest marginal deterrent effect, subject to practical and humanitarian considerations?

The second distinction—general versus specific deterrence—is found in most of the literature. A general deterrent instructs the community at large about the threat of punishment. Thus a penal statute and penal servitude are both general deterrents. Conversely, a specific deterrent deters the individual being punished from subsequent antisocial behavior. Zimring and Hawkins, however, find this latter distinction somewhat spurious. They argue that punishment can be seen as an attempt to deter both all potential criminals and those actually punished.[23]

Despite some terminological confusion, the idea of deterrence is staging a comeback. Nevertheless, Zimring and Hawkins point out that we still don't know much about it:

The net effect of increasing attention and study is something less than a knowledge explosion. There are doubts about both the reliability and relevance of much of psychological experimentation that has been done. The lack of methodological rigor combined with extrapolative extravagance have in many studies produced counterfeit conclusions. There have been modest increments in understanding; but most results have been suggestive rather than definitive. Many questions remain unanswered, among them inevitably those as yet unformulated.[24]

There are a number of reasons for this lack of knowledge. It is understandably difficult to design tests that will yield unequivocal results. For example, it simply isn't possible to compare the deterrent effects of some penalties because the variables that affect crime—not all of which are even known—cannot be controlled in an experiment. Moreover, some penalties that might pack a powerful deterrent are too brutal. But there are other problems.

In part, the diminishment of deterrence is due to the inconsistency of criminologists; many early sociologists thought that deterrence could not be shown to work except in limited instances. (On the other hand, rehabilitation has proved remarkably resistant to researchers' doubts.) In addition, the phenomenon of deterrence is sometimes hard to isolate. An offender may not necessarily be deterred just by the threat of punishment, but also—or perhaps only—by deeply rooted socialization.[25]

There has been a substantial amount of research on deterrence, perhaps as much as on any other correctional question. But aside from some largely insoluble design problems, the research can be characterized in four ways: (1) the work that has been done has focused on only a few sanctions, particularly the death penalty; (2) the findings are often in apparent conflict; (3) commentators, in reviewing the work that has been done, disagree on the interpretation of the findings; and (4) few of the studies are sufficiently oriented to the needs of the policy-maker.

The first problem is remediable—work is being done on new and broader issues.

Conflicting results are not unusual in research, particularly in social science research. But there are a few unusual twists here. Many of the studies, for example, seek to correlate the severity and certainty of punishment with crime rates for given crime categories. But crime rates are notoriously unreliable, perhaps as unreliable as any other data source. From 1970 to 1972, for example, according to FBI Index data, Albuquerque had the highest rates of crime in the nation for cities with populations exceeding 100,000. In 1973 it dropped to 105th. Did all the criminals leave Albuquerque on December 31, 1972? Did the police dramatically become more effective?

Two points can be made about the disagreements in the interpretations of the research. Disagreement about the impeccability of the research designs is to be expected. But a major problem beyond that is that ideological and political considerations may override the clear implications of what research there is. For example, in reviewing some recent literature, Martin Levin points out:

The goal of reducing recidivism conflicts with other values as well. For instance, from what we know about the type of offenders who are most likely to fall into the recidivating group, one clearly could derive the following policy to reduce recidivism: *Incarcerate for the longest terms the youngest offenders, especially if they are black or have a narcotic history.* . . . Conversely, the same findings of social science with regard to reducing recidivism would dictate that judges *ncarcerate for the shortest terms possible under the law whites over 40 who have committed murder or sex crimes!* [emphasis in original][26]

The existence of political pressure isn't debatable. What is harder to understand is disagreement on what the research findings actually are. In two recent articles, two scholars argue along inconsistent lines in referring to the same body of research. Theodore Chiricos and G. Waldo argue that the data from research on the effects of deterrence do *not* show that an increase in the severity of punishment leads to reductions in crime rates, or, conversely, that diminished severity leads to an increase in criminal conduct.[27] Yet in reviewing the same literature, Gordon Tullock, arguing that deterrence—both general and special—works, suggests that some researchers, particularly sociologists, fail to spot relationships because they don't want to:

All the economists I have cited began their studies under the impression that punishment *would* deter crime. All the sociologists . . . began under the impression that it *would not* and, indeed, took up their statistical tools with the intent of confirming what was then the conventional wisdom in the field—that crime cannot be deterred by punishment.[28]

The fourth problem—the lack of research sensitive to policy needs—is also correctable, but only if researchers pay more attention to the evolution of correctional policy. Doing so won't make policy formulation easy. Based only on the results of deterrence research, the derivation of definitive correctional policy is difficult; there are too many other variables. Yet because deterrence has been shown to work in some instances—particularly when there are high probabilities of punishment—it is surprising that it hasn't influenced correctional policy to a greater degree. It shows that the power of an idea—the idea of rehabilitation—is so strong that it has blunted the evidence that deterrence could work. But despite these difficulties, on a common-sense, even visceral, level, we know that most of us are deterred from certain behaviors because of the threat of punishment or social disapproval. There are probably some who are not, and perhaps they are disproportionately represented in the offender population. But because most of us do experience the reality of deterrence, it is surprising that it has had such a low profile in today's corrections.

The reawakening of interest in deterrence is consistent with the reemergence of the theories of retribution and social defense. A retributive formula can readily contain deterrent objectives, as it can contain the aspirations of social defense. In all cases the emphasis is on society, with limiting but secondary considerations for the offender. Only with rehabilitation (and perhaps with the justice model, discussed on pp. 134-135), which owes its origins to the positivistic stress on the individual, is fidelity required; only with rehabilitation are the other "purposes" of punishment largely inconsistent.

Rehabilitation

In 1970, in *Crime in America*, Ramsey Clark encapsulated the prevailing reform movement in the United States: "Punishment as an end in itself is itself a crime. . . . Rehabilitation must be the goal of modern corrections."[29] In 1974 the Citizens Inquiry on Parole and Criminal Justice, chaired by Clark, concluded:

Since there is no agreement on the meaning of rehabilitation, and no one knows what rehabilitates or who is rehabilitated, decisions as to the length of sentence and timing or release based on an assessment of the inmate's rehabilitation are irrational and cruel.[30]

There is a swelling chorus on the evils of rehabilitation. Like Clark, many contemporary observers who championed the concept only a few years ago have now turned on rehabilitation. Rehabilitation is out of fashion today. It's not dead yet, but the literature is littered with death warrants. And there is research support as well. In an exhaustive report, Martinson, Lipton, and Wilks examined myriad treatment variables and find that "nothing works."[31] In other words, the bright promise of rehabilitation has not materialized.[i] What was the promise?

Over the last few decades behaviorists, psychologists, psychiatrists, and social workers have heavily influenced correctional theory and practice.[j] Their focus has necessarily been on individual pathology and the degree to which the offender can be transformed into a law-abiding citizen. Unlike their colleagues in the social sciences, they have been much less concerned with social factors that may influence crime, except insofar as the social context influences individual choice. At their worst, they have contemptuously sought to create laboratory conditions in the prison (or on the street) to seek confirmation of their hypotheses about human behavior. At its most benign, however rehabilitation promised a vision of specialized treatment in the hope of voluntary reformation. In the words of Daniel Glaser, " 'Individualized' treatment in the prison and on parole were seen as keys to both reformation of criminals and the protection of society."[32] To most in the rehabilitation camp, the offenders (along with the rest of us) have had no real choice; their commitments to crime are the consequence of factors over which they have had little, if any, control. But with treatment, conformity is possible, even if choice cannot be restored.

The theory barnstormed correctional practice. Rehabilitation became the byword of corrections. It cannot be overemphasized that corrections nearly became synonymous with rehabilitation in the late 1960s and early 1970s.[k] The only limitation was resources—but where resources permitted, more correctional departments tried to implement the ideals of rehabilitation. The fact that

[i]The terms "rehabilitation" and "treatment" need to be distinguished. By rehabilitation, I mean the theory that holds that the wayward individual can be redeemed, through "treatment," to be returned to society, whether the treatment is premised on actually introducing a change in the offender's character, or simply making him or her fit for reintegration by supplying work and social skills or both. Treatment consists of all the modalities used to rehabilitate.

[j]It is important to note that rehabilitation as a purpose for punishment is not that recent. As early as the 1800s the idea of "correcting" offenders through rehabilitation was fashioned. But as a consuming program for corrections, rehabilitation is a much more recent phenomenon. See pp. 128-130.

[k]As noted on pp. 48-50, rehabilitation as a purpose for corrections has a longer history, but as the term applies to new behavioral treatment techniques, it is a new concept.

nothing seemed to work only led to the argument that the full "kit" of rehabilitative tools had never been used, or that the ideology had not been embraced with sufficient fervor. Charles W. Thomas expresses this "belief" this way:

[C]ontemporary perspectives on treatment and the research on program effectiveness need not be at odds simply because the evaluations of programs so frequently note nonsignificant effects. Both the treatment programs and the evaluation research may be well-planned and executed, but the effects of good treatment programs may be blocked because of influences which are beyond the immediate control of the treatment agents. . . .

Treatment programs in correctional institutions, even though very well-designed and implemented, are very likely candidates for failure unless organizational commitment to the treatment ideology is sufficiently strong that basic alterations in the structure of the organizations is effected.[33]

California came the closest to the ideal. Its rehabilitation forces were the strongest, and they achieved their greatest foothold. Much of the research on the question originated there, and in this sense its erosion can be traced to California as well. In commissioning (and tolerating) research to evaluate the effectiveness of treatment, California produced the most compelling case against it.[34]

Why hasn't rehabilitation worked? There are three central arguments. The first has its roots in one of the main premises of rehabilitation: that individuals can be reshaped to conform to consensual morality if their characterological traits can be rearranged. In other words, treatment—therapy—is supposed to restore the individuals' capacity to "choose," or at least their ability to act as if a choice can be made to conform. But this thinking, arguably, is faulty. Many, perhaps most, inmates have proved impervious to the blandishments of treatment. In part this may be true because of the coercive nature of imprisonment, and even of probation and parole. But given that treatment results with volunteers are also mixed, it may be true that treatment works only with a few. We don't know if this is valid, but it can be no more disproved than the converse can be proved.

The second argument is that treatment cannot work when it is coerced, as it invariably is in the prison. Hence there is nothing necessarily wrong with treatment technology, but given the evidence, it can no more work in the prison than reindeer can thrive in the tropics.

The third argument is more subtle. As in the case of other social experiments, rehabilitation of offenders may have been overextended. When rehabilitation techniques were first introduced, there were some reported successes, even as there are today in some European countries. Perhaps the reason treatment "worked" when it was first tried is because the technology was targeted carefully—it was used with only the most optimal subjects. But as time passed and the rhetoric proclaiming treatment heated up, rehabilitation may have become overused, particularly with subjects for which it was patently inappropriate. Hence when it nearly became the sole means to correct the offender, it had already lost its salience.

The struggle isn't over. Rehabilitation has taken a beating in the literature, but it is still in practice. Many prison administrators still are being admonished to rehabilitate and to enrich their therapeutic programs. Rehabilitation refuses to roll over; a focus on the individual remains. In part this is because a substantial segment of the population sincerely believes in individualized treatment. In addition, the technologies of treatment are too well established, too much a part of our lives, for us to abandon them. The debasement of treatment in the prison always will be viewed by some, perhaps by the majority, as proof only of a lack of will. Hence, although it is in retreat, rehabilitation still exerts some influence for three reasons. First, it is both the philosophical and technical base for indeterminacy—as long as the technologies of individual treatment exist, and as long as we look to mitigating circumstances when we seek to punish, all offenders who do X will not receive Y.

Second, the model remains alive because it is deeply entrenched. Undoubtedly, there are lags among the consensus of criminologists, the consensus of the practitioners, and the consensus of the policy-makers. And in this scheme the public can't even be charted. Most of the public probably believes that Sing Sing still lives and that brutal rapists are manacled together with matricidal maniacs harvesting sweet potatoes. These lags suggest that for all the fulminations of theorists, the rehabilitation model will be with us for a little while longer.

Third, it also fuels two reform movements: reintegration and community-based corrections. In both cases the idea is to reestablish (or establish) ties between the offender and the community—family, jobs, friends, hobbies, organizations, and so on.[1] But the offender somehow must be channeled back to the community and given the means to "reintegrate." Because "treatment" has galvanized such a powerful opposition, the emphasis can be placed on reintegration with a further stress on the role of the community. This is the core position of the National Advisory Commission on Criminal Justice Standards and Goals ("Standards and Goals" Commission).[35] Its elements include the minimization of offenders' "penetration" into the criminal justice system to make their eventual reintegration easier; the dissolution or modulation of the distinctions between exoffenders and the general public; emphasis on exoffender rights; and the use of therapeutic techniques and other programs designed to smooth the offenders' transitions back into the community. Ultimately, however, it is difficult to distinguish this position from rehabilitation because most of the technology used to reintegrate an offender is rehabilitative. The only major difference in reintegration theory lies in its emphasis on the community as opposed to the fortress prison. Theoretically, the community will undergo its

[1]There are differences in emphasis between rehabilitation and reintegration. John Conrad points out the differences in "Reintegration: Practice in Search of a Theory," in *Reintegration of the Offender into the Community* (NILECJ Monograph, June 1973). Washington, D.C.: Government Printing Office.

own soul-searching and change to promote prosocial behavior in the exoffender. But because this ideal is difficult to translate into practice, the rehabilitation of the offender probably will remain the essential method, even though the argument is that it should take place in the city instead of in rural areas. Of course, this in itself implies a host of changes in correctional practice. The result of a reintegrative thrust in corrections might be a very different system, even though the technology would remain essentially rehabilitative.

So with occasional uneasiness, some advocates still argue that rehabilitation can work. They assert that it simply hasn't yet been tried, that not enough resources and talent have been put to work. In *The Future of Imprisonment*, Norval Morris may have made the most powerful and yet careful argument for this approach.[36] He does not argue for "coerced cures" through treatment, but rather for voluntary rehabilitation, which he labels "facilitative." As he and Colin Howard put it in an earlier work: "power over a criminal's life should not be taken in excess of that were his reform not considered as one of our purposes."[37] Morris, like many others, seeks to dissociate himself from the extreme wing of the school—the zealous behavior modifiers. To quote one of them, James V. McConnel: "Somehow we've got to *force* people to love one another, to *force* them to want to behave properly."[38] Morris acknowledges the appropriateness of behavior modification in certain circumstances, but he opposes using any therapies that coerce cures, principally those tied to parole.

Rehabilitation is far from dead. It originally sprang from humanitarian impulses, and as a result it will not be an easy pushover. But perhaps it shouldn't be pushed over. It may be a classic case of losing the baby when the bath water is tossed out. If rehabilitation is taken to mean the attempt to change an offender's behavior through the use of essentially therapeutic techniques, including both individual psychotherapy and group counselling techniques, then, as Martinson argues, there is no dependable aggregate information that it "works." But to assert that rehabilitation doesn't work for offenders as a whole is not the same as saying that it cannot work for some. Even heavy-handed treatment techniques do work for a few. And second, rehabilitation can be defined more broadly to include vocational training programs, education programs, prison jobs that translate into free world job opportunities, and arts and skills training to name a few. And if it is, then it is clear both from the evidence and from a wealth of anecdotal information, that rehabilitation has and can "work." The tar brush that most have put to rehabilitation has been too broad even though the movement itself became a captive of those who believe that the human being can be engineered to conform.

Towards a Unified Theory

If crime appears under so many different guises and in response to such widely varying social conditions, is it to be expected that any single factor, in individual or society can furnish a general explanation or offer a general remedy?[39]

Much of the theory about punishment shares some common terrain. But many of the theories collide at critical points. Nevertheless, the search for unified theory is a perennial interest. For Radzinowicz, retribution occupies a central regulatory role, but like Jerome Hall and H.L.A. Hart, he recognizes that there are many different justifications for different aspects of the punishment process and that as a result no seamless web of theory for punishment is possible. This position is most attributable to Hart, however, who has clearly shown that some of the purposes for punishment are mutually contradictory.[40] But this doesn't mean that any combination of theories is untenable. It is unlikely that any one theory of crime and its causation will hold—the problem has proved far too slippery for such an easy solution. But a combination of purposes is plausible, particularly now that rehabilitation is fading from the scene. In fact, it appears that that is just what is happening.

Where We've Been: The Eras of Corrections

In *Ideology and Crime*, Radzinowicz somberly concludes, ". . . we distrust philosophizing and call for facts. . . . we know there are no shortcuts to the scientific understanding of society or individuals."[41]

There are many histories of corrections; there is no need to redo what is available. What is needed instead is a kind of social, conceptual history of corrections—an identification of the themes and movements that have influenced correctional practice.

I could devote separate chapters to the theories of criminology, the philosophies of punishment, and the technology of corrections. That can't be done here, but the ground must be trodden if corrections is to be taken apart, examined, and put back together again. In this section, I will try to look at the "eras" of correctional practice by examining three dimensions: (1) the prevailing world view of deviance in a given era; (2) the technology available for "punishment"; and (3) the paradigm for correctional practice, which represents a fusion of the first two. This schema will demonstrate the interplay among criminological thought, theories of punishment, and correctional practice. I will emphasize the evolution of ideas, not the chronology of events.[m]

Era 1: Corrections in the Community

Not until the early 1800s did a philosophy of punishment emerge that was based on the idea that pain should be purposively inflicted on the offender because the

---

[m]Throughout I am limiting myself to what we know about the philosophies of crime and punishment and the "practice" of corrections in the Western world, particularly in the United States and Western Europe.

pain had some curative value and that the punishment should be calibrated to fit the crime. Before the flowering of the idea of punishment as a means to some end, deviance was considered a disease or a "pollutant," to use Sutherland and Cressey's term.[42] Social deviance was perceived in much the same way as physical illness: it was a condemnation of the community.[n] Pathology, social or physical, represented disharmony, a failure somehow to keep the gods at bay; and because balance, rhythm, and appeasement were fundamental, the response was extirpation of the disease. Nothing less than annihilation was required; the viability of society was at stake. In short, the technology was brutal, almost entirely informal, and very unambiguous. Only after the early 1800s did the deprivation of liberty, as opposed to corporal punishment emerge as an alternative.

The community was also asked to help in the "cure." The shaman, when confronted with sickness, enlisted the aid of the entire community to heal, to restore a harmonious balance. Often the symbols of the sickness had to be eliminated; the diseased hut and belongings of the diseased might be destroyed. Similarly, if social deviants were not cured by community ridicule and social disapprobation, they had to be erased by other means—perhaps death or exile. Private vengeance played a part as well, particularly when the offense could be processed through standing patterns of socially enforced penalties—leading ultimately to our civil system of reparations.

The resultant paradigm was one of localized, community-based justice. No judicial apparatus or law enforcement mechanisms were needed. Grievous wrongs to the community at large, such as treason or sacrilege, were punished by the entire community. The penalty, whether death or exile, was known and exactingly executed; everyone in the community knew what to do, how to respond. Similarly, wrongs among individuals didn't require public machinery. Vengeance was permitted, even encouraged, in the interests of balance and proportion. And if the offense was intrafamilial, the smaller community of the family, with the full acquiescence of the larger community, used the weapon of social disparagement to return the stray to the fold—or if that failed, left him or her no choice but to be a pariah.

In sum, "justice" was swift, arbitrary, and harsh. Social solidarity demanded punishment, and the means, in insular communities, varied from community to community. The only constant was severity even though some modes of punishment were decidedly more severe than others. Joan of Arc probably suffered more than the pick-pocket who was quickly decapitated. The ideal of punishment as a means of "correcting" the offender, except in the limited instance of the intrafamilial offenses, hadn't been formulated; neither had a theory of crime and its correction.

[n] I use the term "social deviance" because at this time, sharp distinctions were not made between the various forms of antisocial behavior.

Era 2: Monarchs and Puritans

The rise of the monarch's authority created the first "public" system for punishment. Some offenses were now considered to have been committed against the "public"—an abstraction, but nevertheless a legal entity that transcended the victim and the insular community in which the victim and the offender resided. The deviant was still considered diseased, but now the disease was as much an offense to the larger public as to the offender's family and community.

The public's perception was less mystical than in preliterate times: There was little punishment in the names of gods. Moreover, natural harmonies and transcendental balances were less important, less real than the social and political order. The deviant was less a leper in the cosmic order than a threat to good government.

Despite the monarch's authority, the remedies were not much different than they were in earlier times. The technology was still fairly basic:

A detected criminal was either fined, mutilated, or killed, but punishment, as we now understand the term, was seldom inflicted; that is to say, the dominant idea was neither to reform the culprit nor to deter others from following in his footsteps. If a man was killed it was either to satisfy the bloodfeud or to remove him out of the way as a wild beast would be destroyed; if a man was mutilated by having his fore-finger cut off or branded with a red-hot iron on the brow, it was done not so much to give him pain as to make him less expert in the trade of thieving and to put upon him an indelible mark by which all men should know that he was no longer a man to be trusted; if a fine were levied, it was more with a view to the satisfaction of the recipients of the money or cattle or what not, than with the intention of causing discomfort or loss to the offender.[43]

In the United States variations on these brutal themes developed that were peculiar to the New World mentality. Branding was a favorite, witch trials an occasional thrill, and a stocks at every busy corner.

In this simple world, fault—to the extent to which it was assigned—lay with the individual who ignored the moral imperative. Deviance was the product of individual choice and hence was not a constant phenomenon. All that the individual had to do to avoid punishment was to stick to the rules. Those who failed to do so, for whatever reason (and the reasons were largely irrelevant), got nailed—no frills, no tender loving care.

The paradigm that emerged is exemplified by the treatment of the vagrant. Because order and regularity were important objectives, the vagrant posed a problem. The penalty was exclusion. There was no intent to correct, either here or in England, where the courts were established under the monarch's authority. David Rothman points out that the colonists spent very little time developing programs to reform offenders, and further, that they did not expect to eliminate crime.[44] The miscreant simply needed a lesson, and if he or she strayed again, a more severe lesson would be needed.

The era was transitional. The government's role in punishment enlarged and slowly became distinct, for community cohesion was less complete than it was in times of less mobility and permeability. Nevertheless, the emergence of the public administration of justice still did not carry with it the idea of correction. The pieces of a criminal justice system could be dimly seen, but that system still lacked a correctional component. The self-sufficiency of the insular community had begun to erode. Larger systems were needed to fuse communities together in order to facilitate an awakening commerce. Feudalism was nearly dead; industrialization was embryonic. A correctional "system" hadn't been needed; it wasn't yet needed. But it was taking shape, brick by brick.

Era 3: The Enlightenment and the Law of Criminal Justice

Prior to the eighteenth century, random individuals encountered random strictures against random conduct. The only thing that wasn't random was the severity of punishment. The penalties may have varied—whipping for one, branding for another—but all were equally barbarous by today's standards:

Punishments were, in general, as arbitrary and barbarous as the rest of the procedure. They were unequal in application in that the nobility were exempt from some of the most painful and degrading. Some were determined by law or local custom, others left entirely to the discretion of the judges. Even where a punishment was prescribed by law, it could be modified or aggravated by the judge. The only real restriction was that he could not invent a completely new penalty. There was little need of that: existing punishments were cruel and of exaggerated severity, ranging from burning alive or breaking on the wheel to the galleys and many forms of mutilation, whipping, branding, and the pillory.[45]

In other words, people and beasts had much in common, and there was scant belief that the human lot could be improved. The crook wasn't greatly different from anyone else, perhaps just more stupid. Again there was no attempt to correct. If the average citizen couldn't be improved, certainly the offender was a hopeless case. There was, in short, a kind of desperation. Existing feudal institutions had become clumsy and corrupt. The arbitrariness and cruelty of the institutions of criminal justice were manifest. A philosophy of hope was due.

If the past was stuck with tradition and authority for its own sake, the future would have to reject those ideals and substitute a more rational, enlightened order. If the past preserved its barbarity out of superstition and inertia, the future would need inspiration to invent new institutions based on reason and the possibilities of human growth. Men (and to some extent, women) had rights—they were not just servants of the traditional order. Born free, they had been progressively stripped of that freedom by the abuses of feudal institutions; that freedom must be restored. The individual had rights as much as society did, and the tool to secure these rights was the law. The law could be used creatively to erect and then preserve a basic set of human rights against the capriciousness of feudal society. Because all humans were inherently equal, the task of the law was to preserve their equality and freedom by adducing principles that ensured fair and uniform treatment.

The classical theory of crime that emerged from this crucible was a reaction to the brutality of feudal society and, in particular, to the unbridled assaults of feudal institutions on human dignity. The theory's rise was associated with the increasing integration of the social order; systems and institutions were welded together out of the remains of previously self-sufficient communities. The conception was a rational, enlightened scheme of punishments characterized by even and uniform application of rationally conceived laws, but in all cases commensurate with the gravity of the offense. Classical theory promises a penal system emphasizing the "social contract" that binds people and institutions together. Classical theory, in short, springs from a measured and stable universe where regularity flows out of the rational pursuit of happiness. To the extent that crime intrudes on regularity, the "contract" is broken and punishment is necessary—as long as it fits the crime.

Punishment, whatever the form, must necessarily fit the offense, not the offender. There was no theory of individual propensity to crime, nor of individualized treatment. Prior to classical thought, justice had been individualized, not for the protection of the offender but because of the caprice of the punisher. But now order and consistency were paramount: A social contract existed, and if broken by the offender, punishment would be swift and proportionate to the offense. Deviants, because they were free, had chosen to break the bonds that tied them to society—a construct fashioned out of the consensus of freely choosing individuals. In this sense deviance represented a new kind of disharmony—breach of contract. But because "fate" was less of an influence on the conduct of human affairs with the dissolution of feudalism, offenders conceivably could be reintroduced to the social and moral order.

For the first time, punishment was a means to something else: reformation of the individual. For the first time punishment was linked to a purpose for the individual, not just for society. A penalty inflicted to "appease the gods" or "warn" the community of someone's nasty propensities is a more limited tool. While such a "purpose" also might be served in an enlightened penology, beyond those purposes the individuals now stood to "benefit" from their own punishment. The lesson of their punishment would shape the future conduct of the rational actor and others who witnessed the punishment. Therefore the primary purpose of punishment was the restoration of rationality.

The primary tool of an enlightened criminal justice is an enlightened criminal law. The development of criminal codes proceeded under the impress of Enlightenment thinking. The notions of due process emerged in English law, and were soon exported to the colonies. Prominent among its features is uniform application. If one magistrate imposed a sentence of banishment and another the whip, this goal couldn't be achieved. If equality under the law was to be realized, equality of treatment was necessary.[o]

The prison met this criterion, but at the same time, it provided almost infinite variations in the degree of punishment. Offenses of increasing seriousness could be matched by increasingly severe penalties. There had to be more variation than three fingers of the right hand chopped off vs. four. In the prison the range of dispositions—from a day to life—was ideally suited to a graded set of punishments carefully matched to the severity of the offense.

There are many explanations for the introduction of the prison. David Rothman offers the most complete and exhaustive analysis. To him, the arrival of the prison was a major cultural event. He examines the prison in an attempt to derive its social and cultural origins. Why in the early 1800s did society (first in the United States, then soon after in Western Europe) begin to build large institutions to house offenders? Rothman sees a complex picture, for him one of the answers is to be found in the changing perceptions of deviance shaped by industrialization and urbanization.[46] These developments led to disjunctures and discontinuities in the community—the stresses associated with urbanization and the transformations of community life introduced by industrialization profoundly disturbed the tranquility and regularity of preindustrial life. Social deviance was perceived as both cause and effect, and yet at the same time, an occasion for experimentation. Asylums—new communities—could be constructed for those least able to adjust to change, those most in need of regularity. These new communities then could be used as laboratories to discover the means to recapture the cohesion of the past. But the past couldn't be recaptured. Hence the prison of today—no longer a legacy of social experimentation, but a cold leftover—is an institution constantly in search of a purpose. It is used anyway, despite the lack of a clear· mission, because no new social experiment has been conceived to recapture the "good old days." Moreover, we are stuck with these monstrous, costly "laboratories." It's one thing to dismantle a junior high chemistry lab; yet another to abandon 65 acres, millions of bricks, and scores of buildings.[p]

Prior, then, to the Enlightenment, some criminal justice administrative apparatus had evolved and served to administer a rough and ready justice fashioned out of the whims of those in power. It lacked governance from a body of rationally conceived laws, and it lacked a purpose for its punitiveness. The

---

[o]Of course, there was a limit to equality. To the Enlightenment thinker, equality meant a kind of "natural" equality, but it did not mean that differences in rank, station, or wealth were unacceptable. They too were part of the natural order. See Radzinowicz, *Ideology and Crime*, p. 5.

[p]As complete as Rothman's analysis is, one explanation he seems to have overlooked is that the prisons fit the Enlightenment desire for uniformity of treatment, coupled with the "range" necessary to match offense to offender. It is probably true that they were social laboratories as well, as Rothman argues; but these notions are complementary, not contradictory.

Enlightenment era supplied a paradigm that in turn supplied both the law and the purpose for punishment. The object of the law was to ensure uniformity of treatment of citizens who had mistakenly read the tea leaves of pleasure and pain. And the object of punishment, increasingly meted out in the prison, was to deter those who persisted in misreading or those who might be tempted to do so.

Era 4: The Flight from Uniformity

Enlightenment scholars may have seen freely acting citizens abiding by a rational social covenant, but the criminologist in the mid-nineteenth century, under the influence of a kind of biological positivism, saw individuals falling into criminal conduct for reasons beyond their control. Deviance was the product of various "natural forces"—the reversion to more primitive evolutionary behaviors, brain damage, the disorienting effects of mechanized society, or the pressures of an unjust social order. Deviance then was no longer a calculated risk by freely choosing citizens, a willful departure from a smoothly running social order. Instead there had to be reasons why some people—and in particular, certain types of people—failed to internalize social and moral codes. Because deviant populations could be identified, the task was to examine the underlying causes of deviant behavior, and whether those causes were to be found in the social order, the individual, or both.

These views coalesced into a second major criminological school—positivism, which represented the first substantial departure from classical thought. The "bridge" was a kind of "neoclassicism" that encroached on traditional theory by admitting exceptions to the uniformity of punishment. Circumstances could mitigate the punishment or perhaps aggravate it. In other words, punishment could be moderately tuned to fit the unique circumstances of the offense. This is a crucial shift because it suborned judicial discretion, which in turn made it possible to individualize the penalty to change the offender. Pure classical thought that pathology was pathology—it might be "excised" by imprisonment, but it couldn't be transformed into health tissue. The positivists, acting inexorably on their belief that there could be a "science" of the social order as there was for the physical order, poured the foundations for today's corrections. Moral laws existed and could be identified; once deviance was recognized, then, the means to "change" the offender could be devised in order to reattach him or her to that moral consensus.

This perspective necessarily led to a shift in the way the criminal was to be handled. No longer would uniformity of punishment under a set of carefully crafted laws do. There was less reason to punish, more reason to prevent similar behavior in the future. The key to prevention lay in articulating the peculiar characteristics of the offender and then tailoring treatments to remedy the individual deficiencies that were discovered.[q]

---

[q]There are clearly some inconsistent views among positivists. Both the Marxist and the strict behaviorist would deny common roots; but both, for different reasons, should find uniform treatment under the law intolerable.

The technology came in three parts. The first was the scientific method. Society was no longer a mystery: it would respond to analysis in the same way the physical environment had; and crime was no more a mystery than the social order in which it occurred. Cesare Lambrose and other biological determinists sought to identify individuals who were predisposed to crime by personal characteristics they could not control. As G.A. Van Hamel stated, "The classical school exhorts men to study justice; the positive school exhorts justice to study men."[47] And when the biological approach was discredited, other "sciences" were marshalled to carry the banner, including anthropology, psychology, and psychiatry.[r]

A second tool was the criminal law itself. A corpus of law, which had grown up under classicist thinking, reflected a set of ideals about the regulation of society; the law was based on a universal set of irreducible human rights. But to the positivist there was nothing immutable about the law; it was just a tool that was used to ensure the protection of society from the conduct of certain individuals. And as such it could be transformed as needed to match social change.

At the root of positivism lies the belief that the vigorous application of the scientific method would uncover a scientific base for culture and behavior. Once found, it could be used to measure and classify deviance like diseases or chemical elements. As Hans Eyesenck puts it, "Criminality is obviously a continuous trait of the same kind as intelligence or height or weight."[48] The thousands of clinicians, technicians, psychologists, doctors, and other moral change agents that have streamed in and out of the prison for the last few decades owe their invitations to the positivists. Once the nature of an individual's deviance could be measured, the treatment could be tailored to his or her own needs. In short, positivism is less a theory than a technology; people may become positivists not out of any special view of the world, but because they are convinced that there is causality and that it can be empirically verified.

Measurement and treatment were powerful technologies, but a third technology was needed—a laboratory to facilitate experimentation with the other two technologies. The prison first established in the early 1800s (among other reasons to ensure the uniformity the classicists so lusted), could now become, in Rothman's words, a "laboratory for social improvement."[49] Prisons have always been a retort for reformers—they have always afforded reformers opportunities for social engineering. Prisons were needed in the classical era in part because uniformity was desired. Positivists had different objectives, but uniformity was an advantage to the positivists as well because they also had experimental goals in mind. To the creators of the prison, sameness had the advantage of creating an environment for learning; inmates might learn from separation, obedience, and hard work what society had failed to teach them. If this experiment worked, society itself would benefit from the lesson. But the positivists had no plans to change the social order; their targets were the offenders. In the classical scheme the offenders could choose rectitude and hence correct themselves; but to

---

[r]The "biological" approach is staging somewhat of a comeback. See Chapter 4, pp. 61-64.

the positivists, who lacked a belief in free will, offenders could return to society only if carefully crafted therapies could finally make them fit once again.

The correctional paradigm that emerged was not whole; the classical and positivist schools continued to compete. One of the principal avenues of competition centered around theories of punishment. For the positivist, punishment itself was unnecessary. Why punish? Misbehavior was not the offender's fault. For identifiable reasons the offender had simply failed to stick to the social consensus that ultimately governed. If punishment didn't make sense, a change in corrections did. The emerging paradigm, then, was distinctly correctional, not punitive; penal and individual reform—not social reform—was the goal.

Era 5: Social Reform, not Penal Reform

The positivist rebellion has not yet died; it is alive and well in rehabilitation theory. But it was forced underground. Its unrelenting empiricism of the individual fostered a counterreformation. Positivists sought to detach themselves from the agonies and discontinuities of society as if they were transitory perturbations. This view was far too apolitical for many, especially many social theorists. To them, the inequities and conflicts in society were a product not of natural forces, but rather of political exploitation of the powerless by the powerful. They ranged from Emile Durkheim—who perceived crime as an inevitable, logical, and necessary outgrowth of a fundamentally unjust order—all the way to some like Richard Quinney, who almost argue that crime does not exist except as it is labeled by society. In other words, to many social theorists nothing was inherently wrong with the deviant, but something was dramatically wrong with society. These new theorists parted from the classicists because to them free will could not be exercised when political and economic organs discriminated against those who had neither privilege nor opportunity. And they radically diverged from the positivists because they perceived no consensus, only conflict among groups and individuals for shares of the corporate whole. As a result, social theorists eschewed the battery of disciplines the positivists employed to isolate the causes of individual slippage, and came up with their own brand to look at social, rather than individual, causes of crime.

Sociological analysis, from its origins with Durkheim and through a number of scholars including Robert Merton, Edwin Sutherland, and others, has provided a critical mass of theory for criminology until very recently. Sociological theory has driven us to look for the sparks of crime in the community. To some, like Richard A. Cloward and Lloyd E. Ohlin,[50] the argument has been reasonably straightforward: Where you find poverty, ill health, and discrimination, you will find crime because "legitimate" routes to well-being have been closed. To others, social and environmental conditions don't relate in quite so linear a fashion to crime; rather, they form the bedrock for the creation of deviant subcultures that in turn foster crime.[51] And to still others, crime doesn't arise so much from withering social and economic conditions as it does from the "reaction"—the ascription of deviant labels—by the powerful to the "coping" responses of the poor. Yet whatever the theory, most if not all sociologists agree that lurking somewhere in the social order are causative levers—in the family, in social roles, in the relation between the individual and an unjust political order and so on—which, if pressed in the right combination, will shove some into crime. James Q. Wilson articulates this common perspective as follows:

All [sociological theories of crime] sought to explain the causes of delinquency, or at least its persistence. All made attitude formation a key variable. All stressed that these attitudes were shaped and supported by intimate groups—the family and close friends. All were serious, intelligent efforts at constructing social theories, and while no theory was proved empirically, all were consistent with at least some important observations about crime.[52]

What were some of the "important observations"? First, crime could be said to be something more than the consequence of individual impulses and urgings—there are social and economic factors that at a minimum create a context for criminal conduct. Second, some individuals are more prone to criminal conduct, not because of individual differences (although there may be an uneven distribution of criminal propensities), but because of the differential impact of social and economic conditions. And third, the immediate social environment of the individual is probably more significant in shaping criminal motivation than more global and abstract social factors.

These are just a few of the bare elements of the sociological perspective. Yet agreement has rarely been achieved on even these few principles. No comprehensive theory of crime has emerged among sociologists: all that has emerged is a new perspective on an old problem, one that persists because sociologists continue to climb over prison walls.

The social analysis of crime has been the deepest stream of modern criminological thought. Curiously though, most sociological analysis has finessed the prison, or corrections in the broader sense. This doesn't mean empirical work on the prison, probation, and so forth hasn't been undertaken—a vast amount of work has been done on the prison as a social institution. Erving Goffman's *Asylums*[53] is a prime illustration. Yet criminological thought, as informed by sociological analysis, has focused so heavily on crime and its causes that corrections often have been neglected. As a result, sociological thought has had very little influence on the conduct of corrections, except in the limited sense of the prison as a congregation of lost souls. The prisons that the nineteenth century created became wracked with problems and produced no appreciable successes. There were a few "reform movements"; the movement launched in

1870 by the Cincinnati National Meeting actually planted rehabilitative roots.[54] But fundamentally, the prison built in the early 1800s has stayed with us and still serves as the blueprint for the correctional institutions of today. Over the last hundred years, at least until the mid-sixties or so, we may have learned about crime and its causes, but we have learned little from sociology about what to do about corrections.

To some, if society harbored the causes of crime, punishment of the individual for antisocial behavior is anomalous. Ramsey Clark, for example, describes a series of grids consisting of geographic areas of high poverty and low social services, poor housing, inadequate nutrition, and so forth.[55] Superimposed on these grids are the regions of high crime. The causes of crime, Clark argues, are obvious: Crime is concentrated where life is most brutal. But if this is so—if crime is caused by a criminal society that tolerates the brutality of poverty—it is arguably both illegitimate and illogical to punish those who engage in it, because the larger society is the greater offender. To quote Jeffrie G. Murphy, "Modern societies [because of their class inequities] largely lack the moral right to punish."[56]

Not all sociologists think this way. Punishment may be anomalous, but it is necessary nonetheless. Until the social order is tidied up, it still may be necessary to deal with the incorrigibility bred by past and prevailing inequities. So for many sociologists, corrections has a purpose, a kind of bland mixture of social defense and rehabilitation. The sociologists have produced a mound of work, but correctional practice has persevered with its legacy of past reforms. In their preoccupation with social causes, criminologists failed to link theory to practice sufficiently: "Punishment"—well, that's really kind of unfair; "deterrence"—well, that doesn't work, does it?; "retribution"—no, that's decidedly barbaric and unjust; "social defense"—well, yes, until the millenium is reached, I guess; "rehabilitation"—well, now that's something else.

Era 6: The "Disappearance" of Crime

Everything just clanked along until the late 1950s. Old theories were polished, but the crime rates stayed high and seemed to get higher. Then a shift took place. Gresham Sykes puts it this way: "In the late 1950's and early 60's, a distinct change began to make its appearance. . . . Why? [B]y the beginning of the 1970's it was evident that a new strain of thought had entered American criminology."[57]

To some, crime was the product of individual choice. To others it was substantially determined by social and environmental conditions. But to a few it was neither; instead it derived from the social reaction to certain behaviors—in other words, from what it was called or labeled. This new strain was the "interactionist" school—the third major school. It has been most fearlessly stated by Howard S. Becker, author of The Outsiders:[58]

The act of injecting heroin into a vein is not inherently deviant. If a nurse gives a patient drugs under a doctor's orders, it is perfectly proper. It is when it is done in a way that is not publicly defined as proper that it becomes deviant. The act's deviant character lies in the way in which it is defined in the public mind.[59]

Austin Turk also puts it briskly: ". . . A criminal is most accurately defined as any individual who is identified as such."[60]

The "interactionist" rebellion, which reached fruition in the late sixties and early seventies, was itself a reaction—first to the lack of politics in both classical and positivist thinking, and second to the blandness and "liberalness" of mainstream sociological thought. To the interactionist the world didn't just glide along on the skids of a social contract. Rather, people held opposing views and promoted their own interests against those of others. In the interest group struggle for power, the poor and powerless always lose. The most powerful people use the criminal justice process to define crime as that which is committed by those who oppose them.

To quote Sykes again:

According to the emerging "critical criminology," the criminal law should not be viewed as the collective moral judgments of society promulgated by a government that was defined as legitimate by almost all the people. Instead, our society was best seen as a *Gebietsverband*, a territorial group living under a regime imposed by a ruling few in the manner of a conquered province.[61]

A major plank of the interactionist platform is the labeling argument It has been variously stated, but succinctly, the argument is that attaching the label of "criminal" to an offender has the effect of producing "secondary deviance," or subsequent criminal behavior. In other words, deviance is perpetuated as a result of the attachment of the label itself—it becomes a self-fulfilling prophecy.

Interactionist thinking collides with theories that look to genetic, psychosocial, and "individualistic" explanations. These theories tend to presume some fixed nature to deviance, as if what was called deviance was obviously deviant and had always been so. And it differed from the approach of Durkheim and others in that it didn't necessarily assume that crime was universal: Presumably, in a wholly "just" society, one without as much conflict, crime might be dramatically diminished, if not eliminated.[s]

The interactionists are as hard to lump together as the positivists. There are a few constants. For the positivists the proper focus is the individual or the set of variables that, after examination, prove to have "caused" the individual to commit the crime. The variables might range all the way from the genetic through the psychosocial to the environmental. But to the interactionist the crux of the issue lies in the definition of the crime—to the interactionist it is the social framework that "creates" the crime, not the individual. Hence some in this school argue that crime might be reduced substantially if society modified

---

[s]It is true that for Durkheim crime might be "reduced" given certain conditions, but he never argued that it could be eliminated.

its "reaction" patterns. But to still others, "social reaction" may itself be a constant, although the phenomenon to which reactions are elicited may change over time—what was crime to one generation may have been spirituality to another.

The Marxist position on crime is a derivative of interactionist thought. Marx addressed the crime question only incidentally. So it has been left to others to interpret, reinterpret, and re-reinterpret a few of Marx's one-liners in the hopes of fashioning a theory. To the Marxist, crime is a function of class oppression and of labeling.[t] To quote Quinney: "The rates of crime in any state are an indication of the extent to which the ruling class, through its machinery of criminal law, must coerce the rest of the population, thereby preventing any threats to its ability to rule and possess."[62] This thinking tacitly accepts the "labeling" dogma of the interactionists and moves on to define who is doing the labeling—the ruling classes—and for what reason—to oppress and to dominate.

Related to the Marxist and interactionist views is the argument that crime is a general and uniform phenomenon. Asserting that criminal labels are often class-based, the argument is that there is a substantial amount of "hidden crime"—that in fact crime is evenly distributed throughout the population. Punishment, then, is inequitably visited on the poor and powerless.

The interactionist argument that the reaction to an act infuses it with its criminal character is somehow incomplete. Crime almost seems to disappear, or at least it becomes latent in the process of ascription and is brought to life only when some poor devil engages in some behavior that triggers the reaction. Strictly speaking, then, interactionism is less of an "era" than a state of mind; it is more politics than praxis. And this is obviously so with respect to corrections.

The interactionist rebellion held no keys to correctional reform. It may make some difference in corrections if the dynamics of crime were known. But the answer to that question doesn't compel any particular philosophy of punishment. If anything, the interactionist position argues against punishment because it lodges crime's causes with society, which by virtue of its responsibility is stripped of the requisite moral authority to punish. But this argument, not surprisingly, has not deterred states—capitalist or socialist—from punishing.

Era 7: The New Reform of Rehabilitation

It is hard to see how rehabilitation could have been forged from the odd couple of positivism and the more radical wing of interactionism. Yet strangely, that seems to be what happened. Positivism, with its emphasis on the individual, never disappeared although it assumed a lower profile when its most obvious excess—criminal anthropology—was resoundingly refuted. Then with the upsurge of the behavioral sciences in the last twenty to thirty years, a new sophistication

---

[t]"Labeling" is also (more commonly) used to describe the process whereby an offender continues on a deviant trajectory once he or she is labeled as a deviant by society.

cloaked positivist objectives. The intent was no less than to "cure" criminal pathology through treatment. But the new treatment philosophy would never have been received hospitably had not two other conditions been present.

The first was "environmental determinism." If crime can be seen to be the product of harsh social conditions, as Ramsey Clark and others tried to show, then because many of those conditions are beyond amelioration, the offender deserves compensatory treatment. And this is why those interactionists who looked to the social causes of crime fed the humanitarian impulses of the reformers in the 1930s and 1940s. To the engineers of behavior, the inmates were mostly cannon fodder—a captive audience with which to experiment. But to the humanitarian, pained by the degradations inflicted on inmates by society, treatment was a small way of saying, "I'm sorry."

But even this volatile combination of new technology and humanitarian impulses may not have taken off if decades of neglect hadn't left the prisons in such dismal shape. The nineteenth-century reformist ideals that led to the prison's creation had long since been tarnished. The prison had become an anachronism by the late nineteenth century; but lacking alternatives, the correctional system had stayed put for about a hundred years. Reform movements had flickered, only to be extinguished.[u] A new hope was needed—a new technology to deal with the problem. The prison corrupted all who lived in it, and most who did were repeaters. Reform required a new technology, but it also required the broader social support that "liberal" philosophy could provide.

The new technology was the therapeutic toolkit: psychologists, psychiatrists, and social workers clamored for access to the prison to try out new ideas. The three cornerstones were: classification, education-therapy, and a change in attitude measured by psychometrics as well as by subjective judgment.

The basic idea was simple: First, classify the offender by problem and need; next tailor a program to his or her specific needs; and finally, measure the offender's progress towards a possible release date. Prisons remained the same structurally, but programmatically they were changed as they were infiltrated by a swarm of behavioral scientists. Those who entered the gates had a strong vision:

It is the hope of the more progressive elements in psychopathology and criminology that the guard and the jailer will be replaced by the nurse, and the judge by the psychiatrist, whose sole attempt will be to treat and cure the individual instead of merely to punish him. Then and then only can we hope to lessen, even if not entirely to abolish crime, the most costly burden that society has today.[63]

At first, particularly in the late nineteenth century and early twentieth century, the purpose was rehabilitation.[64] But until the emergence of treatment in corrections, the inmate may have needed education but didn't need therapy.

---

[u]Some of these movements even had a rehabilitative thrust, in particular the Cincinnati convocation. See note 54.

Early rehabilitative thinking was not coupled to a deterministic view. Rather, the belief was that "individualized treatment," education in particular, would lead the inmate to render social instead of antisocial choices. But the behaviorists who entered the lists in this century, particularly after the Great Depression, applied a more strict model that stripped the inmate-patient of the responsibility for his or her cure. Only the "expert" could do it:

> If we are to persist in our treatment metaphor, we must see crime as disease, not as a disease. Just as there are many different treatments which we apply according to the nature of the sickness and the requirements and conditions of the individual suffering from it, so must we apply, by analogy, this diversity theory to the problem of criminal behavior and design our treatments accordingly. We must think, exclusively, of individuals who have offended against established precepts and of the treatment appropriate to the individual case.[65]

The prison has continued to punish by confinement and occasional brutality, but the new treatment technology has been grafted to the old methods. It has received lip service from correctional personnel and resources from state legislatures, and hostile rejection by many inmates.

The paradigm of the last three decades is very different from those of prior eras. Seldom has the purpose of corrections been so clear and so unchallenged. Punishment was unnecessary, even vicious; retribution was sadistic at best, especially when offenders lacked the requisite control over their actions; deterrence would not and could not work in an imperfect market—rational choices required rational choosers, and the offender was far too diseased to exercise choice; social defense looked far too much to the community when individual problems could be solved. As a result, rehabilitation became nearly the sole purpose of corrections through the 1950s and into the 1960s. But by then the rumblings of discontent had begun to be heard.

Notes

1. See Norval Morris and Gordon Hawkins, *The Honest Politician's Guide to Crime Control* (Chicago: University of Chicago Press, 1970).

2. David Rothman, *The Discovery of the Asylum* (Boston: Little, Brown, 1971).

3. William Nagel, *The New Red Barn* (New York: Walker, 1973).

4. Herbert Packer, *The Limits of the Criminal Sanction* (Stanford, Calif.: Stanford University Press, 1968), p. 35.

5. Edwin Sutherland and Donald Cressey, *Principles of Criminology*, 6th ed. (Philadelphia: Lippincott, 1966).

6. Ibid., p. 268.

7. Sutherland and Cressey, *Principles of Criminology*, p. 572.

8. John Bartlow Martin, *Break Down the Walls* (New York: Ballantine, 1954).

9. Morris and Hawkins, *Honest Politician's Guide*, p. 112.

10. Sutherland and Cressey, *Principles of Criminology*, p. 287.

11. Nigel Walker, *The Aims of the Penal System* (Edinburgh: Edinburgh University Press, 1966).

12. Nigel Walker in R.J. Gerber and Patrick D. McAnany, eds., *Contemporary Punishment* (South Bend, Ind.: University of Notre Dame Press, 1972), p. 92.

13. Andrew Von Hirsch, *The Justice of Punishment*, report of the Committee for the Study of Incarceration (publication pending).

14. Marc Ancel, *Social Defence: A Modern Approach to Criminal Problems* (New York: Schocken, 1966).

15. Jerome Hall, *General Principles of Criminal Law* (Indianapolis: Bobbs-Merrill, 1947), pp. 550-551.

16. See, for example, Helen Silving, "The Rule of Law in Criminal Justice," in Gerhard Mueller, ed., *Essays in Criminal Science* (South Hackensack, N.J.: F.B. Rothman, 1961).

17. Packer, *Limits of the Criminal Sanction*, p. 49.

18. See Chapter 5, pp. 105-110.

19. Morris and Hawkins in Gerber and McAnany, *Contemporary Punishment*, footnote 29, p. 162.

20. "The Purpose of Prisons," *Newsweek*, February 10, 1975, p. 36. Copyright 1975 by Newsweek, Inc. All rights reserved. Reprinted by permission.

21. Franklin Zimring, "Threat of Punishment as an Instrument of Crime Control," *Proceedings of the American Philosophical Society* 118, no. 3 (June 1974):231.

22. See Johannes Andenaes, "The General Preventive Effects of Punishment," *University of Pennsylvania Law Review* 114 (May 1966):949-983, especially p. 954. See also Andenaes, *Punishment and Deterrence* (Ann Arbor: University of Michigan Press, 1974).

23. Franklin Zimring and Gordon Hawkins, *Deterrence* (Chicago: University of Chicago Press, 1973), p. 73.

24. Ibid., p. 3.

25. See, for example, William Bankston, "Toward a Macro-Sociological Interpretation of General Deterrence," *Criminology* 12 (November 1974):251-280.

26. Martin Levin, "Crime and Punishment and Social Science," *The Public Interest* 27, no. 96 (Spring 1972):102. Reprinted with permission.

27. Theodore Chiricos and Gordon Waldo, "Punishment and Crime: An Examination of Some Empirical Evidence," *Social Problems* 18 (1970):200-217.

28. Gordon Tullock, "Does Punishment Deter Crime?" *The Public Interest* (Summer 1974):107. Reprinted with permission.

29. Ramsey Clark, *Crime in America* (New York: Simon and Schuster, 1970).

30. Citizens' Inquiry Board on New York Parole and Criminal Justice, Inc.,

Prison Without Walls: Report on New York Parole, (New York: Praeger Publishers, Inc., 1975), p. 176.

31. See Douglas S. Lipton, Robert Martinson, and Judith Wilks, *The Effectiveness of Correctional Treatment: A Survey of Treatment Evaluation Studies* (New York: Praeger, 1975); see also Robert Martinson, "What Works?—Questions and Answers About Prison Reform," *The Public Interest* 35 (Spring 1974):22-54; and James O. Robison and Gerald Smith, "The Effectiveness of Correctional Programs," *Crime and Delinquency* 17 (January 1971):67-80.

32. Daniel Glaser, "Societal Trends: From Revenge to Resocialization: Changing Perspectives in Combating Crime," *The American Scholar* 40, no. 4 (Autumn 1971):655.

33. Charles W. Thomas, "The Correctional Institution as an Enemy of Correction," *Federal Probation* 37 (March 1973):10-11. Reprinted with permission.

34. See Robison and Smith, "Effectiveness," pp. 67-80.

35. National Advisory Commission on Criminal Justice Standards and Goals, *Task Force Report: Corrections* (Washington, D.C.: Government Printing Office, 1973).

36. Norval Morris, *The Future of Imprisonment* (Chicago: University of Chicago Press, 1974).

37. Norval Morris and Colin Howard, *Studies in Criminal Law* (Oxford, England: Clarendon Press, 1964), p. 175.

38. James V. McConnel, "Criminals Can Be Brainwashed—Now," *Psychology Today* (April 1970):14.

39. Sir Leon Radzinowicz, *Ideology and Crime* (London: Heinemann Educational Books, 1966), p. 74.

40. See H.L.A. Hart, *Punishment and Responsibility* (Oxford, England: Clarendon Press, 1968), especially Chapter 1.

41. Radzinowicz, *Ideology and Crime*, pp. 127-128.

42. Sutherland and Cressey, *Principles of Criminology*.

43. See W.L.M. Lee, *History of Police in England* (London: Methuen, 1901), p. 10.

44. Rothman, *Discovery of the Asylum*, p. 3.

45. Radzinowicz, *Ideology and Crime*, p. 3.

46. Rothman, *Discovery of the Asylum*, p. 79.

47. G.A. Van Hamel, quoted by Radzinowicz in *Ideology and Crime*, p. 56.

48. Hans Eyesenck, *Crime and Personality* (London: Paladin, 1970), p. 74.

49. Rothman, *Discovery of the Asylum*, p. 107.

50. Richard A. Cloward and Lloyd E. Ohlin, *Delinquency and Opportunity: A Theory of Delinquent Gangs* (Glencoe, Ill.: Free Press, 1960).

51. See, for example, Marvin Wolfgang and Franco Ferracuti, *The Subculture of Violence* (London: Tavistock, 1967).

52. James Q. Wilson, "Crime and the Criminologists," *Commentary* (July

1974):48. Reprinted with permission; copyright 1974 by the American Jewish Committee.

53. Erving Goffman, *Asylums* (New York: Anchor, 1961).

54. See, for example, David Fogel, unpublished manuscript, pp. 29ff.; Negley K. Teeters, "State of the Prisons in the United States: 1870-1970," *Federal Probation* 33 (December 1969): 18ff.

55. Clark, *Crime in America*, pp. 56-67.

56. Jeffrie G. Murphy, "Marxism and Retribution," *Philosophy and Public Affairs* 2 (1973):217.

57. Gresham Sykes, "The Rise of Critical Criminology," *Journal of Criminal Law and Criminology* 65 (June 1974):208.

58. Howard S. Becker, *The Outsiders: Studies in the Sociology of Deviance* (New York: Free Press, 1963).

59. Howard S. Becker, *Sociological Work* (London: Allen Lane, 1971), p. 341.

60. Austin T. Turk, *Criminality and the Legal Order* (Chicago: Rand McNally, 1969), p. 18.

61. Sykes, "Rise of Critical Criminology," pp. 208-209.

62. Richard Quinney, *Criminal Justice in America*, (Boston: Little, Brown, 1974).

63. Benjamin Kaysman, quoted in Sutherland and Cressey, *Principles of Criminology*, p. 65.

64. Fogel; Teeters, "State of the Prisons."

65. H.H.A. Cooper, "Toward a Rational Doctrine of Rehabilitation," *Crime and Delinquency* (April 1973):239. Reprinted with permission.

Part III:
What We Do and
Don't Know

4 Crime and the Offender

Crime and Corrections: The Simple Questions

If a journalist stopped people in the streets and asked them what they most wanted to know about crime and corrections, what would they say? What are some of the simple and fundamental questions that most people ask?

—Is the rate of crime increasing?
—Is there more violence today than in the past?
—What are the causes of crime?
—Who commits what kinds of crime and how often?
—Why shouldn't we lock up offenders for a longer time?
—What should be done about the victims of crime?
—What effects does corrections have on the crime rate?

The principal purpose of Part III is to identify the critical questions about corrections, whose answers would aid us in understanding the relationship between corrections and the rates and incidence of crime. A second purpose—on the assumption that corrections has more than the reduction of crime among its purposes—is to look at the other purposes of corrections. To start, how much do we know about a few of the questions people in the street care about?

The Rates and Incidence of Crime

There is widespread belief that there is more crime today than ever before. This is probably true, but we don't have hard evidence. FBI Index data consistently reflect increases in crime in recent years—11 percent from 1973 to 1974, and 18 percent from 1974 to 1975—but these increases aren't sufficiently controlled for a host of variables—including age distribution, population mobility, reporting distortions, to be accepted as definitive proof. Nevertheless, in 1967 the President's Crime Commission, on the basis of its survey of the data, and controlling for most of the explanatory variables, concluded that, "The number of offenses . . . has been increasing. . . . Most forms of crime are increasing faster than population growth."[1] Yet this report only reflects reported crime increases in the early 1960s. There are some who argue that the "crime wave" is abating—that crime rates have leveled off and even may be declining.[2] (This is a controversial position. See the discussion in Chapter 2.)

Crime may be increasing, but the data on which the arguments are based are notoriously prone to distortion for a wide variety of reasons, most of them political.[3] Unfortunately, victim survey data, which perhaps are more reliable than index data, aren't sufficiently longitudinal to resolve the question one way or the other.

If it's hard to tell whether there is more crime today, can we argue that even if there isn't more overall crime, there may be more violent crime, more predatory crime? For the same reasons, no. All we can say is that there seems to be more. According to FBI Index crime data, from 1961 to 1974 the robbery rate rose 255 percent; forcible rape, 145 percent; and aggravated assault, 153 percent.[4] But again, we don't know how reliable the data are. It is possible that increased reporting of "sensationally" destructive acts has created a belief that such behavior is actually more prevalent. But is what is considered violent just bodily assaults, or property crime as well?

The problem again may lie in reporting; are there more rapes per capita today than, say, ten years ago, or has the stigma of reporting weakened and thus led to an accelerated reporting rate?

However this debate is resolved by academicians and researchers, the public seems to believe that there is more crime—and this in turn becomes a social fact. The result is that the perception of more violence stimulates policy as much, if not more, than the data.

We can't answer all the "big" simple questions; unfortunately, we can't answer many of the "small" questions either. For example, we do have a rough idea about the rate of recidivism in general—about 50 percent—but we don't know what the differential recidivism rate is for various types of crimes and offenders. For example, we don't know who recidivates more frequently, second- or third-time offenders. Nonetheless, what knowledge and theory are available?

The Offender and the "Causes" of Crime

For a long time individuals didn't make any difference. All that mattered was the preservation of society and the covenants upon which it was based. Eventually, however, someone noticed that organisms populated this watchpiece world and, further wondered what made them tick. This interest in the individual naturally led to an interest in individual differences. Criminals have always been perceived as a little different, so they became an object of study, even of fascination. Criminals have remained an object of study in criminology and corrections ever since.

Briefly, what do we know about the causes of crime? One major issue that we haven't decided is what we mean by a "cause" of crime. Ultimately the criminal law is based on the assumption that what causes one individual to steal and another to refrain is each individual's choice. Only by assuming that environmental pressures were not determinative can the law pin responsibility on the individual. This is probably as it has to be, because the presumption of free will—not its scientific verification—is at the heart of the criminal law. Nevertheless, as a rich and supportive environment may encourage (without necessarily causing) excellence, a debilitating environment may encourage (without necessarily causing) crime.

There are three major clusters of causes: biological and psychophysiological; psychological and psychosocial; and socioenvironmental. However the evidence is assessed, it's clear that all the clusters contribute to the crime rate. What we don't know is in what proportion—not only with respect to individual offenders, but in general. We know, for example, that the psychological characteristics of the offender contribute to criminal conduct. And we know that social and environmental factors create a context for the play of individual motivation. Finally, too, we know that some individuals' motivations may be shaped by biological disposition. But again, we don't know what the mixture is or how the mixture works itself out in the offender's peculiar social circumstances.

This set of questions is very political. Psychological factors are accepted as germane, but because they seem largely impervious to change, particularly with the erosion of the rehabilitative ideal, they are becoming increasingly irrelevant. Everyone acknowledges the social and environmental deficits that many face, and everyone admits that these factors can condition social responses. But because only some who are similarly situated engage in crime (or at least are detected in doing so), such factors are obviously not determinative; they may be necessary but not sufficient.

These are controversial propositions, but they don't excite nearly so much clamor as the biological arguments. Some recent studies have shown that biological disposition is related to the incidence of crime. This idea raises hackles, because in the so-called land of opportunity, disability can be social, even psychological, but not biological.

The Statistical Perspective

The criminal has been assessed from the legal, social, economic, biological, and psychological perspectives—in each case with the intent of discovering what motivates and, as such, "causes" criminal conduct. Each perspective has something to offer, but first what are the few simple things we do know about the offender.

Most offenders are young, and most offenses are committed by the young. Of the FBI Index crimes, 48.9 percent are committed by those twenty-two and under.[5] The young also commit 49.6 percent of the violent crimes (homicide, rape, robbery, and assault).

Disproportionately, the offender is black; 35 percent of arrests for FBI Index crimes are of blacks, whereas blacks represent only 11 percent of the total population. There are a host of reasons for this: we will discuss some of them later.

Crime is a market dominated by males, but females are making inroads. In 1960 only 10 percent of the arrests for Index crimes were of women. In 1975, 19 percent were attributable to females, mostly young women.

Most offenders live in big cities. (Of course, that's where the population is concentrated.) Crime, at least insofar as it is reported, is principally an urban phenomenon. Major metropolitan areas, which hold only 73 percent of the population, are responsible for 84 percent of Index crimes. Within the city most offenders reside in slum areas, or at least in areas characterized by urban decay, although increasingly offenders prey in and on the suburbs.

Most offenders are unemployed or at least underemployed. When the economy is sluggish, the same people who contribute disproportionately to the crime rate are those who have the most difficulty finding jobs or are discharged from jobs they might have held.

When it comes to money—which is a function of employment to some extent—most offenders (the ones who get caught, that is) don't have any. Most seem stuck permanently on the lower socioeconomic rungs. There have been some notable exceptions—particularly the recent incarceration of some politicians and political henchmen—but affluence is not common to offenders.

This much is easy. Although there are gaps in our information, we know a fair amount about the social, economic, and demographic characteristics of the offender. But it gets harder after this—the drop in our knowledge is steep. We are confronted by a host of competing, sometimes conflicting, theories about criminal behavior.

The Legal Perspective

From the perspective of the law, offenders are cardboard figures, and almost necessarily so. They are presumed to know the law and further, they are presumed to act on the basis of that knowledge. If an offense is committed, any further inquiry into motivation stops. It is then simply a matter of applying the appropriate legal standards that the offender "willingly" violated. Mitigating circumstances are occasionally taken into consideration, but only if they are "objective"—unemployment, prior offenses, family associations—except when the "insanity" defense is raised, in which case an inquiry into motive is permissible.

The model is simple and easy to apply. The information we have about human nature, as checkered as it may be, clouds this clear, pragmatic view. Offenders emerge as cutouts. Yet whatever else we may know about offenders, this beige view of them prevails in the criminal justice system today; it is, of course, a premise the criminal law is based on.[a]

The law refuses to indulge in psychology, sociology, anthropology, and biology (although judges store some of it in their subconscious) because the inquiry into guilt or innocence must stop at some point. The criminal law is designed to make a fair but not exhaustive examination into the question of guilt, and then arrive at an appropriate disposition. To the extent to which causative, motivational, and attitudinal considerations muddy this process, the law becomes a less balanced and less precise tool, however much it may appear to be more humane. The argument in favor of the blinders that the law dons is that equality of treatment is the ideal, despite its infrequent realization. This fundamental (and often elusive) fairness is what the advocates of the "justice model" for corrections are seeking—a streamlined correctional experience shorn of pretense and posturing.

The Biological Perspective

In 1968 Richard Speck murdered eight nurses. Since then a number of commentators have used the "Speck" scenario to construct arguments about criminal motivation premised on biological or innate predisposition.[b] The arguments have hardly been universally accepted. One of the reasons is that we have been and remain in an era when innate differences are ideologically undigestible. Yet there is some recent research, of considerably more sophistication than Lombroso's, which is hard to ignore. In most cases the work that has been done seeks to restore the role of heredity to the prominent position it once enjoyed. Hutchings and Mednick's study will illustrate.[6]

The observation that led to the research was that children of persons who had been convicted of crime were themselves more involved in criminal conduct. The purpose of the research was to disentangle, to the extent possible, the relative impact of genetic or hereditary influences from environmental ones. The research was undertaken in Denmark, where a central repository of vital statistics facilitates this kind of inquiry. Adoptive parents were matched in an experimental group of adoptees (who had been removed from their natural parents while very young) who had criminal, natural parents. A control group consisted of adoptive parents of adoptees whose natural parents manifested none of these traits. As a result, the "environment" of the two groups of

---

[a]A more sophisticated version of the "legal offender" can be found in retributive thinking, particularly in the report of the Committee for the Study of Incarceration. In this conception, offenders are presumed to know, or at least to be responsible for, the consequences of their behavior; a calculus of "just deserts" is then applied to fix a penalty.

[b]It was first suggested that Speck was an "XYY"—that he suffered from a chromosomal abnormality—because he bore a physical resemblance to the XYY "type." It turned out that his chromosome makeup was normal.

adoptees should have been about the same—that is, all adoptees were exposed to noncriminal adoptive parents. The results revealed a significantly higher incidence of criminality among children whose natural parents had criminal records.[c]

So what do we do with this? First, it's important to stress what the results do and do not show. They do not show that a propensity towards crime is an inherited trait. At best all they show is that there may be a biological or psychophysiological predisposition to crime. Second, there are numerous methodological problems with the research, not the least of which is the problem of "contamination." The only constant the researchers could guarantee was to match adoptees with adoptive parents to secure rearing environments that were not influenced by biological parents. Attempts were made to match the myriad other environmental variables—such as income, education, and parental attitudes and behaviors—but that task is very difficult. Nevertheless the biological variables turned out to be significant. Given this, and assuming that additional research confirms the results, further examination of offenders must incorporate whatever insights and evidence can be marshalled about biological predisposition. This examination is already being undertaken.

Saleem Shah and Loren Roth, both affiliated with the National Institutes of Mental Health, have looked at the evidence.[7] Their first mission was to dispel the doubts (and fears?) of other investigators about the possible role of biological and psychophysiological variables in the matrix of causative factors. Other investigators, according to Shah and Roth, mistakenly attributed more explanatory breadth to biological and psychophysiological factors than the proponents of such research claimed for themselves. Few have argued that biological phenomena "explain" or "cause" crime. Rather, biological evidence must be mixed with other evidence to devise a formula with sufficient explanatory power, and even then hard-to-quantify phenomena like "free will" can confound the theory. We don't know how to create such a formula yet, but it is a key task if we are to discover how biological and psychophysiological variables interact with social and environmental ones.

Shah and Roth also point out a major research design problem. In assessing "criminal predisposition" it is difficult to separate tendencies toward specific criminal conduct from tendencies that may increase the exposure of the offender to apprehension. For example, alcohol not only may reduce inhibitory responses, thus making a person more liable to engage in crime, but it also may make the actor more inept, and hence more likely to get caught. In addition, biological influences must be measured against cultural standards of deviance. If abnormally high levels of testosterone can "cause" assaults, could lower levels "cause" draft evasion? On the labeling question, Shah and Roth comment:

[c]The children of parents who had criminal records and who were raised by "normal" parents had a crime rate of 21 percent. Children of "normal" parents who were raised by "criminal" parents had a crime rate of 11.2 percent. See Hutchings and Mednick, "Registered Criminality," p. 226.

We do not wish to imply that many behaviors likely to be officially labeled as crimes are the product of neurological difficulties. We are suggesting that individuals belonging to population groups at greater risk for perinatal and birth complications and resultant neurological dysfunctioning, who are further exposed to unfavorable social environments during their lives, in general, would be expected to display high rates of deviant behaviors likely to lead to criminal labeling.[8]

The final question goes to application of biological evidence about crime. First, what predictive use do the data have? Shah and Roth point out that the data's predictive value is low; past behavior is a much more reliable indicator of future crime than any biological characteristics.

Second, given that we can show biological and psychophysiological influences, are there prevention possibilities? Shah and Roth assess them in conventional medical care categories: primary prevention (focused on the general population, with a view toward the amelioration of conditions that provoke antisocial behavior); secondary prevention (early detection of potential cases); and tertiary prevention (focused on those who manifest the disorder). Theoretically, much could be done in the way of primary prevention to improve the conditions of birth, nurturance, and socialization, presumably in turn nourishing law-abiding tendencies. But as with other social and environmental conditions, the "leverage" to make improvements may be lacking. Secondary prevention poses two problems. First, even assuming that the disorders could be detected, what would we or could we do about it? Only rarely have we fancied internment for the potentially dangerous. Second, there is the risk of self-fulfilling prophecy. It is possible, nonetheless, that in carefully validated experiments certain techniques might be developed to deal with clearly detectable disorders.

Finally, it is possible to treat some "biological" offenders with chemotherapy and rehabilitative programs. Apparently several successful treatment approaches have been developed, some of which are identified by Shah and Roth.[9] The issues raised by this type of program are many. Whereas there are "prevention possibilities," most of them are fraught with practical and political difficulties. But again, given the chill cast over treatment programs in corrections, successful treatment programs might not fare any better than unsuccessful ones. Ultimately, the questions may have to be resolved through politics rather than through research. At the moment, however, if Shah and Roth are right, we don't know enough to do more than frame better research questions. They conclude their assessment on this tepid note:

Our objective has not been to emphasize the organismic factors in opposition to social and environmental variables, nor to pit nature against nurture in the continuation of an outmoded debate on an incorrectly posed issue. Rather, since the phenotypic characteristics of an organism are the result of continuous interactions between the genotype and the environments to which the genotype is exposed, we have emphasized that more adequate information about organismic variables is necessary for a better understanding of human behavior—including socially deviant behavior.[10]

The Economic Perspective

Economics as a tool of explanation has been used in criminology in three main areas: cost-benefit research, research on deterrence, and research related to deterrence.

   Cost-Benefit Analysis. As prosaic as it often is, cost-benefit analysis often yields insights into the functioning of a system—that is, irrespective of what the system says it does and what it promises it will do, based on where it puts its money, what does it really do? This type of analysis, then, can illuminate the actual behavior of an industry. For example, it can show what effect the government monopoly has, the underevaluation of prison-produced goods and services, and the "overconsumption" by society of correctional services, and so forth. And it can also suggest what are the costs and benefits of engaging in crime.

   Does Crime Pay? To the economist, the criminal isn't much different from anyone else, save that he or she has chosen a morally reprehensible career. In all other respects offenders are presumed to be rational decision-makers, just like the rest of us. If doing X maximizes net returns, minimizes loss, and doesn't generate externalities, then the rational person will do X. This syllogistic formula applies to the criminal as well as to anyone else. Hence if crime "pays" fiscally and/or psychologically, it isn't surprising that people engage in it.[11] And this is especially true if comparable, legitimate income-producing jobs aren't available. William E. Cobb illustrates the points in his study of theft. After accounting for the risks of crime—the probability of the loss of earnings through imprisonment, and the psychological deprivation of incarceration—the profits usually exceeded what could be earned through law-abiding enterprise. To use his words, "Further study is needed, but these conclusions indicate that thieves, as a group, are making the 'right' choices."[12] Although it should be added that if legitimate income-producing opportunities are available and will yield as great or greater return, it follows that the thief will become a respected businessman.

   The appeal of economic analysis lies in this utter simplicity of approach. The investigator can avoid both the murky swamps of social and environmental causation and the political pitfalls of biological and psychophysiological motivation. Beyond this, of course, there is a great deal of truth in what economic analysis contributes to the overall picture.

   Deterrence. The economists' message about deterrence is: "Don't get all tangled up in sophisticated proofs; optimizing individuals, everybody, including crooks, will respond to opportunity and stimuli in roughly the same way." Hence if the "gain" in the prospective "hit" is outweighed by the price, which is a function of its absolute pricetag—for example, ten years—and the likelihood and speed of its imposition, the prospective criminal won't become one, at least this time. As a result, economic analysts have weighed the available research on deterrence, done some of their own, and concluded, like Morris Silver, that "Taken as a whole, the evidence convincingly demonstrates that crime rates are reduced by higher probabilities of punishment."[13] This seems rather simple, understandable, and common-sensical; the contribution economics has made, among other things, is mostly to legitimate common sense. Nevertheless, not everything fits common sense. For example, the certainty/severity debate continues.

The classical position, introduced by Cesare Beccaria, was that certainty was more important than severity. In recent studies by economists this position has come under close scrutiny. Gordon Tullock, for example, suggests that for simplicity of analysis the two aspects be considered as interchangeable: he suggests that a one-in-one chance of serving a year in prison, and a one-in-one-thousand chance of serving ten years be viewed as equivalent—the method should be to multiply the probability of apprehension by the severity of sentence.[14] (This argument, of course, assumes fungibility between one year and ten years—which is highly dubious.)

The importance of this issue is that it may determine whether resources are better spent in improving the probability of apprehension (by bolstering law enforcement) or by providing stiffer punishment (by bolstering corrections). In any event, to date, the studies that have been done comparing the relative importance of severity and certainty have not been conclusive; there has been a tentative verification of the greater importance of certainty, but at least in relation to homicide, Maynard Erickson and Jack P. Gibbs suggest that there is a minimum level of certainty necessary, above which increases in severity of punishment will have a commensurate deterrent effect.[15]

The most important contribution of economists might not lie in their research, but rather in the perspective-broadening impact of their formulations. To think of criminals as businesspeople, scions of a major industry, isn't refreshing, but it offers insight into criminal motivation that can be only keelhauled out of much of the analysis offered by other disciplines. It is true that there are distinct "limits" to the economic analysis of crime. For example, there may be some criminals who are as shrewd as many other businesspeople, but they may be far outnumbered by those who engage in crime for the not-so-rational reasons of hunger, politics, drugs, desperation, or stupidity.[d] Yet to look at criminals as industrialists and crooks as shopkeepers is to gain a new perspective—the most obvious implications of which lie in the area of crime prevention. When government seeks to deter businesses from antisocial behavior, it creates disincentives so that the calculus of profit and loss must be readjusted constantly. The same can be done in crime control by "hardening the target"

---

[d]I am aware that the formulations of some economists, particularly Tullock and Becker, make room for some of these causes, but it is not generally customary in economic analysis.

and by beefing up deterrence. It is surprising that so little attention has been given to crime prevention technology, and to the more conscious use of deterrence, given the low probabilities in trying to change individuals.

Unfortunately, what economics gives with one hand it may take with the other. Crime prevention may be desirable in theory, but it can be astronomically costly. For example, in a study of improved police surveillance of the New York City subway system as a crime prevention tool, it was found that crime could be reduced, but at a cost of about $35,000 per felony prevented.[16] In addition, Edward C. Banfield has estimated that the installation of antitheft devices in new automobiles costs about $5000[e] per theft prevented.[17]

The Social Perspective

If "economic" criminals are decisive, rational allocators of costs and benefits, "social" criminals are shivering masses of silly putty. The image is that of hapless, would-be criminals waiting for the right combination of social and environmental circumstances to propel them into crime. Hence, as in the case of other characterizations of offenders, the image slides into caricature. Yet, also as with the other approaches, there are kernels of truth.

From the social perspective, some individuals are so beset by grinding social and environmental afflictions that crime becomes either a "logical" response or at least a conditioned one. Of course, room is left, at least by most commentators, for the play of individual motivation, and even in some cases, for biological and psychophysiological propensities. But the main focus has been the identification and explication of those social and environmental factors most conducive to criminal conduct.

Social theory is variegated. It ranges from the relatively simple and straightforward to the profoundly obscure. But in all cases the key variable appears to be the development of attitudes and values in those who engage in crime that are different, in some sufficiently significant sense, from those shared by the majority. For example, Marvin Wolfgang and Franco Ferracuti argue, in *The Subculture of Violence*,[18] that the emergence of a set of subcultural values can actually encourage attitudes and behaviors that vary from the dominant culture—a phenomenon called "differential association" by some.[f]

In all cases these attitudes and values are shaped and maintained by the peculiar interactions of the individual offender and his or her intimate social

[e]Note, though, that the absolute figure $5,000 is meaningless without comparing it to the "costs" of the theft—what if the theft "costs" the owner and society combined over $5,000?

[f]Daniel Glaser adds to this notion the idea of "differential anticipation" by wedding the subcultural values created by "differential association" with the opportunities that some possess to engage in crime when legitimate routes to cash and security are closed. (Personal Communications)

interactions, coupled with debasing life circumstances. Yet as James Q. Wilson has argued, no single variable in the social and environmental matrix can be shown to be a significantly causative variable—and this includes race, income, and employment status.[19] Even Sutherland has conceded that poverty isn't causative; further, segregation can't be wholly causative because when the Japanese in the United States were subjected to discrimination, they did not respond with a rash of criminal conduct. Where we end up, then, is with some provable associations between certain socio-environmental-demographic variables—such as race, low income, slum living conditions, deficient education, widespread unemployment, and high rates of reported crime—but no dispositive correlations. Nevertheless, these associations have led sociological interpreters to develop themes to explain how the impact of these conditions presumably lead some offenders into antisocial behavior.

What we have, then, is not a theory but a series of conceptually related arguments. Most of the arguments are very plausible, but we don't know enough to pare away the probative from the speculative. We simply cannot explain why only some similarly situated individuals offend and others do not. It's not similar to the situation with biological and psychophysiological variables—they seem associated, but standing alone they don't explain crime.

There are plenty of good reasons why we should know more about the causes of crime than we do. But there is still a dilemma when it comes to application: as a society we simply haven't demonstrated that we are willing to do much about these "causes," even if we could prove that they were determinative. It may be true, for example, that the disintegration of the family is directly related to the incidence of crime, but what can effectively be done about this by any agency, much less by corrections? At a more abstract level, what if we know that the odds of criminal engagement by an individual rise rapidly if a fixed set of social contacts aren't available? Could we somehow supply them to everyone?[g] As Norval Morris says, "It is trite but it remains true that the main causes of crime are social and economic. The question arises whether people really care. The solutions are so obvious. It's almost as if America wished for a high crime rate."[20] It's not all that bleak. Some moderation of the most harsh and inequitable conditions is possible, but what would be the marginal impact on the crime rate? We don't know. Crime rates often appear to fluctuate with certain gross indicators such as widespread unemployment, but beyond these crude measures we don't have much to go on. But even if we knew more, what would we do about it? Could we or would we restructure society so dramatically that the social and economic jaws that snap at the heels of the most disadvantaged among us could be wired shut? Yet beyond these "obvi-

---

[g]Of course, there are some things that can be done—allowing conjugal visits, funding exoffender programs, and so forth—but it is doubtful that these programs would have more than a marginal effect.

ous" solutions, the problem with most sociological theory is that it stays at the diagnostic level—it is very difficult to translate into prognosis, and even more difficult to apply to correctional policy and practice.[h] This is sharply stated in Wilson's treatment of criminological theory when he says about it, ". . . none could supply a plausible basis for the advocacy of public policy."[21]

The Psychological Perspective

If offenders are neither the products of social forces nor the pawns of politics, they might be sick—the only thing left is the medical model. By this I mean an approach that presupposes that offenders are diseased and can somehow be cured by a mixture of expertise and technology. In practice, of course, treatment hasn't been the last resort but the preferred choice. In recent years the assumption has been almost universally made that the offender was deficient or diseased and hence could be cured through appropriate treatment. This subject has been covered elsewhere. The point here is that despite the repudiation of rehabilitative corrections, and even admitting that the arguments of the therapists have been overstated, there is some explanatory power in the model. It may be that the bulk of offenders are not sick; in fact the medical model may be wholly inappropriate for them, even destructive. But this doesn't mean that there aren't characterological differences between some offenders and nonoffenders, differences that might be altered with carefully tuned interventions. It may still be that some offenders are in fact so bent out of shape that they can be said to be sick. And there is some evidence, largely outside of corrections, that some treatment modalities work. These include some forms of chemotherapy—for schizophrenia, for example—retreat center programs and Alcoholics Anonymous for some alcoholics, and some of the human potential therapies. Perhaps these haven't or can't work in the prison, but they might work in the community.[22] Even Martinson concedes that treatment might work—all he says is that we can't prove it.[23] The danger here is that treatment will be driven underground by the passions of those who abhor it. The intent to change the offender on the assumption that there are deficits that can be resupplied may not change. Instead, it will assume another mantle and bore in again, most probably in the community. There's nothing necessarily wrong with this—dogmatism in opposing treatment may be in error as much as dogmatism in promoting it. Yet it would be nice if the issue could be defused so that the proper place for treatment in corrections, if any, can be found.

---

[h]Arriving at a definitive description of the causes of crime as social and economic, however, would allow us to abandon strategies that are aimed at reducing the crime rate to utopian levels. It is possible to succeed in reducing crime enormously, but given such a perspective, the price might be higher in social and economic changes than we are willing to pay.

A More Policy-Oriented Approach

Each of these perspectives contributes something to an understanding of offenders, even if no coherent theory has yet emerged. The difficulty, however, with typologies of the offenders in terms of the disciplines that have engaged them is that the resulting interpretations are often insufficiently related to policy. There are other ways to analyze offenders that might be more amenable to policy formulation.

For statistical purposes, for example, we need to know much more about offender careers, correlations between certain kinds of crimes and certain offender characteristics. Ideally, a matrix could be constructed that would look something like Figure 4-1. If we could fill in even some of the cells for each offender and then collate the information, we would know a lot more than we do now. Unfortunately, there are very few cells that we can complete confidently. For example, we have very little data to tell us whether there is a progression in seriousness in crime for most offenders.[i] Further, we don't know at what point along the dimension of seriousness most offenders launch their careers; in short, we don't know who does what when, where, how, how often—and least of all, why.

The matrix is something more than a commodities tally. If we could complete most of the cells, we could reassess available strategies for law enforcement, crime control, and crime prevention. For example, as Wolfgang's cohort study suggests, criminal careers don't necessarily escalate in seriousness. There are some, Daniel Glaser included, who doubt the utility of grading offenders in terms of the seriousness of their offenses. It isn't that it can't be done. It can. And it isn't that it wouldn't be nice to know if all crimes, or the crimes of some identifiable crooks, were declining in seriousness. The problem that some have is that to measure crimes by some arbitrary standard is to strip such an enumeration of crimes of their policy salience. A property crime is different than a crime of physical violence, even if each had the same seriousness score and, hence, should elicit a different policy response—a response that might not be forthcoming if the nature and circumstances of the criminal act were disguised by the act's seriousness ranking. If this is so—as we might find out if we completed the matrices—we might ask corrections only to reduce the seriousness of subsequent criminal activity rather than futilely seeking to stamp it out altogether. In addition, the matrices would make it possible to assess the impact of major social interventions designed to reduce the crime rate. If, for example, a program were touted to reduce burglaries in a given geo-

---

[i]One major exception is Marvin Wolfgang, Thorstein Sellin, and Franco Ferracuti, *Delinquency in a Birth Cohort* (Chicago: University of Chicago Press, 1972), which indicated, somewhat surprisingly, no increase in seriousness as criminal careers "progressed."

	Murder	Drugs and drug-related offenses	Property crime less than $X	Property crime greater than $X	Crimes to the body: Class 1	Crimes to the body: Class 2	Crimes to the body: Class 3	Crimes of violence
Age								
Sex								
Residence								
Education level								
Employment status								
First offense								
Second offense								
Third offense								
Multiple offenses								
Time elapsed from time of last offense								

Figure 4-1. Suggested Offender Matrix.

graphic area, it would be theoretically possible to use the matrices to judge the program's impact.[j]

Crime also can be lumped into categories that are more amenable to specific policy responses. Existing classifications are simply catalogues dependent on historical circumstances. They don't give much guidance to those who want to better match crime prevention control efforts with the most optimal targets.

Daniel Glaser, in "Criminology and Public Policy,"[24] suggests a classification of four types of offenders:

1. Adolescence Recapitulators. Glaser points out that most adolescent crime is episodic, often experimental. Moreover, even among those who engage more extensively in criminal activity, few patterns emerge. For some, however, patterns do begin to emerge. As Glaser says:

[j]The "displacement effect" would still have to be accounted for: whether an effective burglary prevention program in Oakland merely shifted the burglars to San Francisco. See also the study of subway crime in New York; Chaiken, Jan M., Michael W. Lawless and Keith A. Stevenson, *The Impact of Policy Activity on Crime: Robberies on the New York City Subway System* (New York: New York City Rand Institutes, 1974) as reported in *Crime and Delinquency Literature* (March 1975).

Those categorized here as "adolescence recapitulators" continue to repeat the not highly specialized predations and group escapades of their adolescence. This category encompasses most youthful and a few somewhat older but unchanged inmates of correctional institutions. They differ from others in our society in the duration and difficulty of their transition from childhood into a stable adulthood, but the difference is a matter of degree, since adolescence for most people involves some deviance and discontinuity in socialization. Eventually most of these offenders support themselves primarily by legitimate jobs rather than by predations, and the remainder shift into one of the other types of criminal careers [described below].[25]

2. Subcultural Assaulters. Glaser offers no succinct definition for this category, save what the term itself and the theory behind it convey. He does argue, though, that this kind of crime should be accepted as a "social fact," in the sense in which "its rates are a function of the attribution of collectivities."[26] In other words, there seems to be a relatively fixed amount of violent crime that seems relatively impervious to public intervention.

3. Addicted Performers, Addiction-Supplying Predators, Organized Illegal Sellers, and Private Illegal Consumers. In this fascinating litany, the central point that Glaser makes is that the criminal law is almost useless in preventing this behavior, presumably because it stems from urges that are not easily controlled. He articulates some general principles:

(a) Any effort to prohibit the sale of goods or services in wide demand creates a highly attractive business opportunity for persons without scruples about violating the law.
(b) Police and other public officials as representatives of the general public are frequently reluctant to enforce rigorously any laws directed against practices that much of the public condones.
(c) Competition among illegal businessmen is not regulated by legitimate agencies, but by acts of violence, so that such businesses usually employ or are controlled by predatory criminals.
(d) Offenders whose crime is the provision of services to private users can seldom be apprehended.[27]

He also adds fifth and sixth principles, which Cressey has documented extensively:

(e) Techniques successful in and capital procured from illegal selling are used by the illegal sellers to acquire businesses previously operated legitimately.
(f) Any law widely violated seriously impedes other law enforcement by overloading law enforcement agencies and promoting disrespect for them.[28]

Predators: Avocational, Crisis-Vacillating, Quasi-Insane, and Vocational. This is a catchall: Glaser includes hitmen and peculating employees under the same rubric. The list is inclusive, but there is a common element, which is that

[T]hese professionals are the offenders most frustrating to law enforcement agents. Policies for public protection from such predators may gain effectiveness by analyses of the life histories of these offenders, using the perspectives of the sociology of occupation and noting the similarities in values and skills of professionals in legitimate and illegitimate pursuits.[29]

Glaser's typology is a significant advance over bunching all offenders together as members of a depraved band. His effort might be augmented by a somewhat sharper, more policy-relevant delineation of some types of crime. The list that follows is not a substitute for the existing criminal code, but rather a list of some types of crime that, arguably, should be dealt with differently than they are with existing criminal codes.

1. **Victimless Crime.** This kind of crime includes prostitution, consenting adult sexual activity, the private use and consumption of chemicals, and private, small-scale gambling. Consistent with many reform proposals, such activity does not necessarily represent a threat to the fiber of the Republic and hence, soon may be decriminalized.

2. **Random Property Destruction.** This kind of crime includes vandalism, breaking and entering without theft and so forth. Most of this activity is associated with adolescence, but the distinction may be spurious. Irrationally destructive behavior doesn't necessarily cease at age eighteen. It may be true that juveniles smash school windows, but it is also true that some conventioneers wreck hotel rooms at their annual conventions.

3. **Systematic Property Destruction.** This category includes systematic activities of groups to destroy property either as a means of demonstrating a principle or to protect the group or organization from the use of property or information against them. Hence infrequent but premeditated raids on Selective Service agencies would be included, as would the shredding of files by governments and corporations.

4. **Property Theft.** This conventional category includes all thefts by burglary, embezzlement, employee peculation, extortion, and so on. It should be divided into two subcategories: episodic and systematic, and public response should be adjusted accordingly. No distinction should be made between a burglary of $1000, an embezzlement of $1000, a "bunko" game taking $1000, the extortion of $1000, bad paper written for $1000, employee theft of $1000, or executive fudging on expense accounts worth $1000.

5. Selling Dangerous Chemicals. This category includes all pushers of chemicals that have been definitively proved to be dangerous to health and well-being, including possibly narcotics, hallucinogens, uppers, downers, and alcohol and tobacco.[k] All sellers of these substances, to the extent to which they pose equal threats to human health and well-being, would be subject to penalty. The point is that the sale of the stuff is a different act than its consumption.[l]

6. Violent Crime. This category—which includes robbery, assault, rape, homicide, and so forth—represents the major focus of past, present, and undoubtedly future crime control technology. These acts are not equally serious and hence, as in conventional classifications, differentiations should be made among the various types—for example, a barroom brawl would not be considered as serious as the murder of a policeman.

7. Economically Motivated, Organized Crime. The target here is organized crime—systematic activity designed to gain unfair or illegal advantages by monopolistic practices, threats, bribes, conspiracy, price-fixing, product tampering and devaluation, and false and fraudulent advertising, and so on. Hence, if our crime control efforts are effective, the Mafia chieftain will occupy the same cellblock as the corporation president who knowingly peddled contaminated mushrooms, *if* the economic and social harm is equivalent.

8. Violations of the Public Trust. The criminal law is effective to the extent that those affected by it perceive it to be just. Violations of public trust by elected officials and others occupying public fiduciary positions should constitute a separate category, suggesting that different criteria might be used in judging and punishing offenders. It is obviously difficult to erect cost-benefit models for violations of public trust to make them comparable to other measures of "seriousness," but the widespread damage done by such violations warrants their inclusion as a separate category.

The ultimate test of both the punishment to be given and the degree to which crime control policy should be focused is the degree of "seriousness," as measured by social harm inflicted by each of the offenders in each of the categories. (I use the term "social harm" the way economists use the term "social cost.") By applying this or similar measures with appropriate sophistication, the criminal law might be made a more precise instrument.

---

[k]To some, including alcohol and tobacco in this list is unrealistic, if not absurd. But if the test is damage to health and well-being, it is equally absurd to omit these substances from the list even though it is highly unlikely that their sale or use will ever be criminalized.

[l]This is an example of the need for conceptual completeness. My personal view, as expressed by Thomas Szasz in *Ceremonial Chemistry* (New York: Doubleday, 1974), is that the criminal law is the inappropriate tool to deal with chemical use and dependency, but it is nevertheless an appropriate category in this enumeration.

The "Offense"

We obviously need to know more about the offender. But we also need to know more precisely the relative social damage of various offenses. The choice of one focus over the other characterizes society's approach to social control. Consideration of the offense leads logically to an analysis of the criminal law and the means by which society defines some behavior as criminal, and by implication, other behavior as law-abiding. In the sections that follow we will take up some of the important issues in this discussion.

The Nature of the Criminal Law

There is a long-standing debate over whether the criminal law is a manifestation of "natural" principles or simply the product of cultural perceptions and attitudes at a particular time. An abstract discussion isn't needed, but some aspects are worth considering.

The Relativity of the Definitions of Crime. There is no need to reargue the point: what is called a crime to one culture may not be the same to another—this is one of the things we know. But we also know that what we call crime, or what we treat more punitively, isn't always the most socially damaging behavior. Is the social cost greater when one person robs another of $1000, or when a corporate executive engages in price-fixing that ultimately costs the public $1 million? Which is more socially corrosive—when a twenty-two-year-old unemployed bricklayer gets a suspended sentence for a first arrest for theft, or when an executive of a multinational corporation beyond the reach of the criminal law bribes officials of other countries with lavish sums?

It is not only that the definitions of crime vary over time, but that the conduct that is defined as criminal at any time may not exact as much social harm as conduct that is not criminal—or that is treated with comparative leniency if it is criminal. As a result, the argument is that the criminal law is easily transformed into an oppressive tool, and as such may be stripped of its foundations.

This is essentially the position of the radical movement in criminology. The argument is neatly summarized in *Struggle for Justice:*

Actions that clearly ought to be labeled "criminal" because they bring the greatest harm to the greatest number are in fact accomplished officially by agents of government. The overwhelming number of murders in this century has been committed by governments in wartime. Hundreds of unlawful killings by police go unprosecuted each year. The largest forceful acquisition of property in the United States has been the theft of land guaranteed by treaty to Indian tribes, thefts sponsored by the government. The largest number of dislocations, tantamount to kidnapping—the evaluation and internment of Japanese Americans during World War II—was carried out by the government with the approval of the courts. Civil rights demonstrators, attempting to exercise their constitutional rights, have been repeatedly beaten and harassed by police and sheriffs. And in the Vietnam War America has violated its constitution and international law.[30,m]

But now what? If the radical analysis is accurate, what follows? Probably one thing is that when inequities in the law are perceived, any shred of law-abidingness in some offenders—not members of "privileged" classes—may be lost. It is reminiscent of the cartoon that appeared shortly after ex-Vice President Spiro Agnew was allowed to plead no contest to criminal charges: An inmate behind the bars shouts, "Get me Agnew's lawyers!" The resulting disrespect for the law is obvious; ultimately, the crime rate may increase because of the weakening moral consensus.[31] But what about the inmate survey data, such as Jonathan Casper's,[32] which suggests that the vast majority of inmates do *not* object to either the economic or the political order as they perceive it? Lacking a political posture, it is unlikely that their criminal behavior was influenced by political considerations. This doesn't mean that our society isn't inequitable, but that it may not be perceived as such by most offenders. There are two other points.

First, what would happen in corrections if the criminal law were transformed to reflect degrees of social harm more accurately? A new "class" of offenders would be created. And if they weren't flushed out of the system into special programs designed for them, what would corrections do with them? Most of the conventional correctional weaponry has been designed for persons about whom certain assumptions have been made—for example, that the average offender lacks will power, intelligence, and discipline. Accordingly, correctional programs have been designed to supply the missing moral and emotional components. But if a new class of inmates shows up—a group for which the old assumptions don't necessarily hold—would we still seek to change the new offender, to quicken middle-class moral impulses somehow? It's doubtful. After all, those very middle-class morals may have served to excuse the offender's past behavior. Nor is it likely that we would seek to punish in the same way, or for as long, as we punish those whose crimes exhibit the lack of "backbone" that corrections commonly seeks to implant. It's one thing to put the burglar away for a flat five years, but quite another to incarcerate the labor official who raided the pension fund. The latter, after all, has supposedly "learned a lesson" by the very fact of conviction.

---

mTony Platt adds, in "Prospects for a Radical Criminology in the United States" (*Crime and Social Justice* [Fall/Winter 1974] :2):

> In accepting the state and legal definition of crime, the scope of analysis has been constrained to exclude behavior which is not legally defined as criminal (for example, imperialism, exploitation, racism and sexism), as well as behavior which is not typically prosecuted (for example, tax evasion, price fixing, consumer fraud, government corruption, police homicide, etc.). The most serious crimes against the people, as the American Friends Service Committee has noted, have been neglected.

Corrections in this scenario could hardly remain the same. It is very likely that the prison would be used less, and that the community could be more imaginatively and boldly used as a correctional site. Miscreants who bribe are more likely to be welcomed back into their communities than those who steal, even if the amount of social harm is the same.

The second point is more subtle. If the definitions of crime were radically revised to better calibrate punishment with the gravity of social harm, what would be the effect on crime rates? Is it likely that the overall "amount" of crime recorded and processed would slightly increase, at least temporarily? All the "new crime," essentially white-collar in nature, might be more systematically swept into the criminal justice system. This might be a very desirable result, but it doesn't augur a massive crime wave. If law enforcement resources remain the same, there is a limit to the amount of crime that can be found. And certainly it wouldn't portend a lack of law enforcement attention to "traditional" crime. It is doubtful that police will ignore rapes, murders, and burglaries to snoop in corporate boardrooms. It may be that resource limitations would slightly decrease the intensity of the law enforcement focus on so-called common crime, but mayhem in the streets still won't be tolerated. So even if the test of social harm was more central to law enforcement, the conduct that the radical criminologist argues is discriminatorily suppressed is likely to remain high on the list. Conceding (in fact, favoring) the social desirability of a criminal law concordant with a calculus of social harm, the argument that the poor and disadvantaged are oppressed by the criminal law loses its force. It just leaves us with another problem—what do we do about people who engage in conduct that is labeled socially harmful in any culture? There is violent crime: people do get mugged, raped, killed, and savaged by other people, not just in corporate boardrooms, but on the streets. To acknowledge that the definitions of crime are relative—and further, that the criminal law has been oppressive—may help us reform it, but it won't get rid of rapacity. Nor will it rid us of the fear of crime.

Decriminalization.

Most of our legislation concerning drunkenness, narcotics, gambling, and sexual behavior is wholly misguided. It is based on an exaggerated conception of the capacity of the criminal law to influence men and, ironically, on a simultaneous belief in the limited capacity of men to govern themselves. We incur enormous collateral costs for that exaggeration and we overload our criminal-justice system to a degree that renders it grossly defective where we really need protection— from violence and depredations on our property.[33]

This, as espoused by Norval Morris, is the central argument in favor of decriminalization. Hans Mattick, a criminologist at the University of Illinois, estimates that "victimless" crime accounts for at least 40 percent of all arrests.[34] Presumably, if the criminal law were less of a busybody, it would scoop up fewer people who are unpromising candidates for corrections. A host of questions accompany this formulation: Will decriminalization result in less warranted social control, in more or less street crime?

Decriminalization is an aspect of the larger issue of the relationship between the criminal law, crime, and corrections. The larger issue has been debated frequently among the various schools of criminological thought. To the positivists, for example, because the law represents a discernible moral consensus, it can be used imaginatively to create the conditions to reform those who stray from that consensus. To the interactionist, the law is also a tool, but for the more powerful to suppress the less powerful. Irrespective of these competing philosophic positions, the footings for the decriminalization movement are two: First, that when there is social change, there will be an imperfect fit between a society's moral consensus (to the extent that it can be identified) and the criminal law; and second, that certain behaviors, whether or not injurious to society, are simply insensitive to legal prohibition. The lack of fit is often the result of a lag in the law as it may reflect society's moral perspective. If this is so, and some behaviors are decriminalized because they no longer violate the social consensus, corrections should benefit; it will not be saddled with those who have only violated an arid proscription that lacks a moral correlate. The same can be argued for behaviors that are decriminalized because the criminal law is largely ineffective in curbing them. Corrections should benefit by escaping the responsibility for correcting someone whose behavior is incorrectible.

The Constancy of Crime. Kai Erickson, in *Wayward Puritans,*[35] examined the records of Salem, Massachusetts, prior to, during, and after the witch trials. Prior to the witch trials the citizens of Salem seemed to be most concerned about strangers in their midst, social and occasionally private improprieties, and carousing in the streets. Banishment, the use of the stocks, and whipping were common remedies. Within a very few years those same citizens were concerned about only one thing: protecting the community against possession by the devil. When the fervor of the community abated and the witch hunts came to an end, the same citizens once again became exercised about such things as drunkenness, fornication, and strangers in their midst.

Erikson's thesis suggests that, irrespective of the labels attached to behavior, and further irrespective of the "content" of crime, the amount of crime remains roughly constant. His study, however, was retrospective and the data were incomplete. Some more recent work by Alfred Blumstein and Jacqueline Cohen seems to be supportive.[36] In examining imprisonment rates in the United States, controlling for population, they found remarkable stability in imprisonment, except for the years of World War II (explainable perhaps by the conscription of many who otherwise might have been members of the prison population). The authors also cite Norwegian data spanning an eighty-five-year period. Again stability of punishment is found, although it is less consistent than in the United States.[37]

Erikson's work suggests that the amount of deviance in a given culture is roughly constant (although the level may vary from culture to culture) and is thus largely immune to social intervention. If this is true, efforts to reduce the amount of crime substantially may be futile or marginal at best.[n]

Of course, even if the theory is valid, it isn't all despairing. First, the margin for change may still be significant. A demonstrable reduction of 10 percent in the crime rate would represent a substantial monetary savings, as well as savings of a number of lives and limbs. Second, because it is the amount of deviance, according to Erikson, that is supposedly constant, crime might be reduced if behavior otherwise treated as criminal were handled by other social control systems. Third, the theory leaves room for interventions that might reduce the seriousness of crime. Deliberate use of deterrence, and effective prophylactic measures, might diminish truly serious crime, leading at worst—if the theory is valid—only to increases in less serious crime. Fourth, the constancy of crime shouldn't lead to nihilism in the treatment of those apprehended. Instead, frank recognition that crime is in some sense a constant might free us (and the necessary resources) to better the conditions of confinement and treatment.

"Hidden Crime." Related to arguments about the constancy of crime is the argument that crime is uniformly spread throughout the population, but that only some criminals are apprehended—particularly those least able to prevent their apprehension. Accordingly, it is further argued that criminologists have had the wrong focus: instead of looking for factors that cause some to be criminals, they should examine the selection processes which nail down only part of the population to bear the cross. Eugene Doleschal has reviewed much of the literature, drawn from European, Canadian, and U.S. sources.[38] He illustrates his case with Swedish and Norwegian data. For example, a random sample of 950 boys between the ages of nine and fourteen in Stockholm revealed that 92 percent of the boys had committed at least one offense, or an average of four offenses each, and that more than half acknowledged at least one serious offense. Among the significant conclusions that Doleschal reached were that delinquents known to the police were more definitely engaged in delinquency compared with the average, and that very few of the offenses were cleared by the police. In the Norwegian study, great variations were found in self-reported crimes between rural and urban areas, but little variation between educational and class levels.[39]

There is strong dissent. For example, Martin Gold interviewed 600 boys and girls (aged thirteen to sixteen) living in Flint, Michigan. Fifty-one questions were asked about activities such as trespassing, vandalism, lying, hitting a parent, stealing, drinking beer, arson, smoking, taking a car, fornication, and carrying

[n]Of course, this may be simply a problem of observation. Because different societies will spend roughly the same amounts of energy "suppressing crime," there appears to be a law at work, which is "supplying" society's quota of deviants.

weapons.[40,0] Gold concluded that *"while official records are selective in a way which exaggerated the relative delinquency of lower status boys, they nevertheless approximate real delinquent behavior."* [emphasis in original][41] Nevertheless, Doleschal asserts in his summary that

The majority of the studies show that the middle and upper classes are just as crime-prone as the lower classes. This finding, however, is contradicted by other studies and remains controversial. All studies, however, agree that official statistics greatly exaggerate the amount and seriousness of crime and delinquency among lower socio-economic groups.[42]

So where does this leave us? If it is true, as Doleschal and others argue, that the incidence of crime is largely uniform throughout the population, then either (1) the causes of crime cannot be entirely social and environmental; or (2) if social and environmental conditions are causative, they aren't the same for everyone. As far as Doleschal is concerned, at least regarding poverty, "This discovery may force the abandonment of the standard belief that poverty is the main cause of crime."[43]

On balance, Doleschal's conclusion may be overstated. Wolfgang's cohort study revealed widespread criminal behavior, but he found that crime was not nearly so uniformly spread among the races and the various socioeconomic strata as hidden-crime theorists suggest. Certain criminal behaviors were more strongly correlated with blacks and some with whites within the larger cohort. Hence the cohort study hardly supports the hidden-crime thesis. Moreover, if its findings are accurate, it conflicts with the implication drawn in many of the hidden-crime studies that all crimes are evenly distributed among socioeconomic groups. On the contrary, the study demonstrates that many offenses are disproportionately distributed in the population, thus agreeing with Nils Christie's observation that "We are all criminals, but most of us only to a very small extent."[14]

Labeling and Interactionism. A final theoretical position related to the "offense" is interactionist theory, discussed earlier in Chapter 3. There is no doubt that the public's response, more particularly the response of more influential publics, shapes some criminal conduct. The interactionist position is sound, to a point. The youngster who hurls a board through a window in frustration and rage is said to be a delinquent. The lawyer who, after a bad shot, hurls a golf club through a window in frustration and rage is said to be having a bad day. To take the argument much farther is to leave it dangling. All behaviors aren't mindless and motiveless—the social setting can't provide all the content of deviance.

---

[0]To study concealment, Gold interviewed a criterion group of 125 youngsters about whose delinquencies reliable information had been obtained (without the children's knowledge); 72 percent appeared to be telling everything that had been obtained through informants previously, 17 percent appeared to be concealing information, and the rest were questionable.

Yet the theory has explanatory power. Among other things, it shows how culturally relative our definitions of deviance can be, and as a result, should compel a continuing examination of the relevance of criminal labels to the needs and tone of contemporary society. Unfortunately there is no one accepted articulation of the theory. In its extreme form it leads to a corollary: Punishment is illegitimate because society is illegitimate. In its more modulated form, the argument is that punishment must be tempered because of its oppressive nature. In its mildest form the argument is that while some punishment may be necessary, largely for social defense, it must be recognized for what it is—not only discriminatory and inequitable, but possibly criminogenic because it attaches labels to offenders that they in turn seek to fulfill.

Leaving aside the forms of the argument, what does it tell us? It tells us that society is wracked with conflict—and we might agree with that. It tells us that deviance is relative—and we might agree that it has qualities of relativity. It tells us that the powerful use labels of deviance to suppress those without power to secure their own power—this too is possible. And it argues that the ascription of criminal labels to offenders somehow leads them to follow criminal careers—and there is some support for this argument. But now what? If it is the response that creates the crime, there may be some things we can do to modify the responses, but without restructuring society, the opportunities for substantial change are limited. Second, although we may precisely identify the selection factors that operate to apprehend and punish only some people, what can we do about them? If, as the interactionist argues, the dominant culture labels certain acts as disagreeable, how do we convince that culture to look at those acts as somehow agreeable? To do so we have to slide into a swamp of values. This can be done—and should be—but to expect rapid change is unrealistic.

In reality these arguments may be much ado about very little. The interactionist position has power because it is a resonant counterpoint to those who argue that crime is wholly the product of "those warped other people," and to those who deny the "warping" effects of culture and environment. It is true that society defines only some acts as criminal and that acts that are so defined just happen to be those more frequently committed by "them." And it is also true, to a degree, that attaching a criminal label to some individuals tends to track them into criminal careers. But beyond these kernels, the theory is far from a complete explanation of the phenomenon of crime.

So in the final analysis, this theory does not leave us much to do. It looks at society as a machine that unfalteringly chews up some of us. Then it describes, sometimes very cannily, how (and sometimes why) the machine goes about its work. But it doesn't explain all of crime and it doesn't tell us what to do about it. And corrections is given a very tough job—"correcting" the machine's output. Then it tells us that when corrections is done correcting, it will nevertheless release its graduates into the same culture that labeled them in the first place, with the additional handicap of having to wear the label everywhere.

A Coda on Theory

Beneath the abstractions of theory lie some important observations:

- At least some definitions of crime and deviance are relative
- "Lags" in the reformulation of the criminal law can lead to profound disrespect and perhaps even disregard of the law
- Crime (or more accurately, deviance) may be a sufficiently universal function of culture, and hence unrelenting attempts to eradicate (or unfettered assaults on human dignity in seeking to control) crime may affect crime rates only marginally
- Some criminal behavior may be relatively uniform throughout the population, and hence one proper focus of criminology is to identify the selection factors that visit punishment on only some
- The ascription of criminal labels to some may encourage further criminal behavior.

Notes

1. See The President's Commission on Law Enforcement and the Administration of Justice, *Task Force Report: Crime and Its Impact—An Assessment* (Washington, D.C.: Government Printing Office, 1967), p. 40.

2. See, for example, Alfred Blumstein and Jacqueline Cohen, "A Theory of the Stability of Punishment," *Journal of Criminal Law and Criminology* 64, no. 198 (1973):206.

3. See "Crime Not Rising, but Figures Are," *New York Times Review of the Week*, Part IV, col. 5 (April 10, 1966), p. 2; and Michael E. Milakovich and Kurt Weis, "Politics and Measures of Success in the War on Crime," *Crime and Delinquency* 21 (January 1975):1-10.

4. "The Crime Wave," *Time*, June 30, 1975, p. 10.

5. These and the following statistics are taken from Federal Bureau of Investigation, *Crime in the U.S., 1973* (Washington, D.C.: Government Printing Office, 1974).

6. Barry Hutchings, Sarnoff A. Mednick, Fini Schulsinger, Jerry Higgins, and Brian Bell, "Registered Criminality on the Adoptive and Biological Parents of Registered Male Adoptees," in Sarnoff A. Mednick, ed., *Genetics, Environment, and Psychopathology* (New York: American Elsevier, 1974), p. 21.

7. Saleem Shah and Loren Roth, "Biological and Psychophysiological Factors in Criminality," in Daniel Glaser, ed., *Handbook in Criminology* (Chicago: Rand McNally, 1974), pp. 101-173.

8. Ibid., p. 129.

9. See, for example, ibid., p. 151.

10. Ibid., pp. 152-153.

11. A.J. Rogers gives a comprehensive treatment of the subject in *The Economics of Crime* (Hinsdale, Ill.: The Dryden Press, 1973).

12. William E. Cobb, "Theft and the Two Hypotheses," in Simon Rottenberg, ed., *The Economics of Crime and Punishment* (Washington, D.C.: American Institute for Public Policy, 1973), p. 30.

13. Morris Silver, "Punishment, Deterrence and Police Effectiveness: A Survey and Critical Interpretation of the Recent Econometric Literature" (City College of the City University of New York), a report prepared for the Crime Deterrence and Offender Career Project, 1974, p. 30.

14. Gordon Tullock, "Does Punishment Deter Crime?" *The Public Interest* (Summer 1974):107.

15. Maynard Erickson and Jack P. Gibbs, "The Deterrence Question," *Social Science Quarterly* 54, no. 3 (December 1973):551.

16. Chaiken, Jan M., Michael W. Lawless, and Keith A. Stevenson, *The Impact of Police Activity on Crime: Robbers on the New York City Subway System* (New York: New York City Rand Institute, 1974), as reported in *Crime and Delinquency Literature* (March 1975):29.

17. Edward C. Banfield, *The Unheavenly City Revisited* (Boston: Little, Brown, 1974), p. 207.

18. Marvin Wolfgang and Franco Ferracuti, *The Subculture of Violence* (London: Tavistock, 1967).

19. James Q. Wilson, "Crime and the Criminologists," *Commentary* (July 1974):48.

20. See "The Crime Wave," *Time*, June 30, 1975, p. 17. Reprinted by permission from *TIME*, The Weekly Newsmagazine; copyright Time, Inc.

21. Wilson, "Crime and the Criminologists."

22. See note j, page 70.

23. See Robert Martinson, "What Works?—Questions and Answers About Prison Reform," *The Public Interest* 35 (Spring 1974):32-54.

24. Daniel Glaser, "Criminology and Public Policy," *American Sociologist* (June 1971):30-37.

25. Ibid., p. 34. Reprinted with permission.

26. Ibid.

27. Ibid., p. 35.

28. Ibid.

29. Ibid., p. 36. See also M. Lewis, "Structural Deviance and Normative Conformity: The 'Hustler' and the Gang," in Daniel Glaser, ed., *Crime in the City* (New York: Harper & Row, 1970).

30. American Friends Service Committee, *Struggle for Justice* (New York: Hill & Wang, 1971), pp. 10-11.

31. See Wolfgang and Ferracuti, *Subculture of Violence*; and William Bankston, "Toward a Macro-Sociological Interpretation of General Deterrence," *Criminology* 12 (November 1974):251-280.

32. See Jonathan Casper, *Criminal Justice—the Consumer Perspective*, an NILECJ publication (Washington, D.C.: Government Printing Office, 1972).

33. Norval Morris, "Crimes Without Victims," *New York Times Magazine* (April 1, 1973), p. 11.

34. See "The Crime Wave," *Time*, June 30, 1975, p. 18.

35. Kai Erikson, *Wayward Puritans* (New York: John Wiley & Sons, 1966).

36. See Blumstein and Cohen, "Theory of the Stability of Punishment," pp. 198-207.

37. Ibid.

38. Eugene Doleschal, "Hidden Crime," *Crime and Delinquency Literature* 2 (October 1970):546. See also Roger Hood and Richard Sparks, *Key Issues in Criminology* (London: World University Library, 1970), especially Chapter 1.

39. Doleschal, "Hidden Crime," pp. 558-559.

40. Martin Gold, quoted in ibid.

41. Ibid., p. 555.

42. Ibid., p. 567. Reprinted with permission.

43. Ibid.

44. Nils Christie, "Scandinavian Criminology Facing the 1970s," *Scandinavian Studies in Criminology* 3 (1971):121-149, especially p. 126.

5

The Transformations of Correctional Practice

The Perennial Prison

Whether the focus of criminology has been the offender or the offense, corrections and the prison as we know them have been with us now for about 150 years. And neither the system nor the prison has changed much. There have been some changes—for example, parole is more widespread today,[a] as is probation, and a few tools like diversion and more sophisticated treatment techniques have been added. But at its roots the correctional system and the prison have remained essentially the same.

The prison may have been with us for decades now, but its rationale—its theoretical basis—has undergone numerous transformations: from social showcase to brutal pen to a playground for therapists. Throughout this time, except at its inception when it was a direct offspring of theory, the prison has rarely "fit" the theory about it. The situation is even more complex today.

What theory we have varies so much with practice that something has to give. In the past what "gave" was theory, but the pressures to retread penal practices may be so strong today that practice may have to give. We know that the prison incapacitates, and we suspect that it doesn't rehabilitate, but we don't know how much deterrent or incapacitative effect it has. We know that parole is often a velvet fist, but we hang onto it because we don't know what else to do. Finally, we know that sentencing strews inequities all over the landscape, but we are reluctant to eliminate the "human factor" in it.

The fact that few breakthroughs have occurred hasn't slowed the various reform movements. The pressures for change are strong, and they affect nearly every aspect of correctional practice. What are these reform pressures, and where are they taking corrections?

Sources of the Pressure for Change

Sentencing

Marvin E. Frankel has written, ". . . the almost wholly unchecked and sweeping powers we give to judges in the fashioning of sentences are terrifying and intoler-

---

[a]At the turn of the century only 10 percent of prisoners were paroled; today nearly 70 percent are released. See Martin B. Miller, "At Hard Labor: Rediscovering the 19th Century Prison," *Issues in Criminology* 9 (Spring 1974):91-113.

able for a society that professes devotion to the rule of law."[1] Any discussion of corrections must include a discussion of sentencing. No other activity within the criminal justice system, save possibly initial police discretion, is so important to corrections. Whom the judiciary chooses to send to corrections is what corrections must deal with—it has no choice. Judges are often not amenable to reform from the outside; they want to run their own show. And they exercise great power in legislative circles. As a result, some of them, perhaps a majority, will resist any diminution of discretion. Sitting on an elevated bench, holding a gavel, with people standing and sitting at your whim is one of the less humbling experiences. Nevertheless, the pressures for reform are there, and they seem to be building. There are a number of major assaults on sentencing practices.

Discretion. The first is related to the substantial disparity in sentences given for similar crimes. Wide judicial discretion has always been a feature of the criminal justice process. But as the disparities and resulting inequities become more visible, they become less tolerable. Table 5-1, drawn from *Struggle for Justice*, illustrates the point.

Race. Our prisons are disproportionately filled with blacks and the young. Table 5-2 documents the point.

According to Erik Olin Wright, based on current data, "[D]uring a given year, one out of every 3 to 4 black men in his early 20's spends some time in prison, in jail, or on probation, compared with one out of every 15 white men in the same age group."[2]

Of course, many people believe that more blacks are imprisoned because more blacks commit crimes. But is there evidence? Blacks are arrested in numbers roughly proportionate to their representation in the prison population.[b] This may mean that judges don't disproportionately send blacks to prison, but blacks also stay longer, meaning (1) judges may be more prone to sentence blacks to longer terms than whites for like offenses; (2) that discrimination is practiced in parole; and/or (3) blacks commit more serious crimes. But even if blacks are arrested out of proportion to their number in the population, it doesn't mean that they commit more crimes; it may just mean that they get arrested more frequently—there may be a host of invidious factors that produce the disproportionate arrest rate. This question, then, like so many others, is one we can't resolve on the basis of available evidence. As Wolfgang and Cohen conclude in *Crime and Race:*

We do not know with certainty the actual amount of crime among whites, Negroes, Puerto Ricans or any other group. We do know that persons of all

[b]The percentage of blacks arrested for what the FBI lists as violent crime is four and one-half times greater than for whites. See Federal Bureau of Investigation, *Crime in the U.S., 1973* (Washington, D.C.: Government Printing Office, 1974).

Table 5-1
Discretion in Sentencing

S.R.T.

Age: 25. *County:* Escambia.

Offense: Principal in first degree to robbery.

Circumstances: Did aid, abet, or counsel another individual to rob four business establishments of $90, $400, $793.78, and $500.

Weapon Used: Subject drove car; was not directly involved.

Sentence: Twenty years. Four commitments of twenty years, each to run concurrently.

Prior Felony Convictions: None.

C.E.A.

Age: 28. *County:* Escambia.

Offense: Robbery.

Circumstances: Did make an assault upon one male individual at Junior Food Store, steal, take, or carry away money currency of the U.S.

Weapon Used: None indicated in report.

Sentence: Life.

Prior Felony Convictions: One.

C.E.B.

Age: 20. *County:* Escambia.

Offense: Robbery.

Circumstances: Robbed male individual of $18.52.

Weapon Used: Knife.

Sentence: Life.

Prior Felony Convictions: None.

L.T.

Age: 18. *County:* Dade.

Offense: Robbery.

Circumstances: Three commitments:
  1. Did make an assault upon a male and a female, and by force did steal a purse containing $13, I.D. cards, charge plates, and one wallet containing $10 and I.D. cards.
  2. Did rob one male individual of cash in the sum of $7.
  3. Did rob one male individual of one pistol and $3 in cash.

Weapon Used: None indicated in report.

Sentence: Four years, one commitment of two years and two commitments of one year each, to run consecutively. Credit for 567 days jail time.

Prior Felony Convictions: None.

J.R.S.

Age: 21. *County:* Hillsborough.

Offense: Robbery.

Circumstances: Did steal from one male individual cash, wallet, and watch of the value of less than $100.

Weapon Used: None indicated in report.

Sentence: Five years. Credit to be given for 142 days jail time.

Prior Felony Convictions: One.

M.E.A.

Age: 18. *County:* Dade.

Offense: Robbery.

Circumstances: Robbed male individual of $12.

Weapon Used: .38 caliber revolver.

Sentence: Five years. Credit for 50 days jail time.

Prior Felony Convictions: None.

Note: Florida law provides a sentence of two years to life for robbery at the discretion of the judge. These examples, assembled by the Prison Reform Committee of the Florida Bar Association, compare differing sentences for similar crimes.
Source: American Friends Service Committee, *Struggle for Justice* (New York: Hill & Wang, 1971), pp. 126-128. Reprinted with permission.

Table 5-1 (cont.)

E.D.	L.L.C.
Age: 43. *County:* Orange.	*Age:* 28. *County:* Hillsborough.
Offense: Robbery.	*Offense:* Robbery.
Circumstances: Did make an assault upon one male individual and steal $1,300.	*Circumstances:* Did by force take away from one male individual cash of value less than $100.
Weapon Used: None indicated in report.	*Weapon Used:* None indicated in report.
Sentence: 35 years. Credit for 123 days jail time.	*Sentence:* Seven years. Credit for 112 days jail time.
Prior Felony Convictions: Two.	*Prior Felony Convictions:* Three.

groups commit many offenses that are unrecorded. We cannot be sure of the degree of seriousness of even the recorded crime without further study. Only from arrests do we know the race of offenders, yet arrests in any year represent only about 30 percent of the index crimes recorded.[3]

This is a nagging problem. Assuming that blacks disproportionately commit crimes, the next question is, How much so? The black-white arrest rate for Index crimes is roughly 5:1, controlling for population; the same is true for prison populations. But can we second-guess the criminal justice system? Victim surveys will help second-guess index crime rates, and hidden-crime studies also help, but most people admit only to minor crimes. The fact is that we can't replace the records of arrest and conviction with anything except another law enforcement system. But given an accurate crime reporting system, it would be possible to weight crimes according to seriousness, and then determine from the rates of commission of crimes (according to race) whether the black contribution to a weighted crime rate is equal to the number of blacks in prisons.

Table 5-2
Incarceration Rates per 100,000 Population, 1970

Age	Black	White
Under 18	24	3
18-24	1013	171
25-44	622	108
45+	161	29
Total	457	64

Source: Data derived from U.S. Bureau of the Census, *Census of the Population, 1970,* Final Report PC (2)-4E, "Persons in Institutions and other Group Quarters," pp. 5-6; and *Statistical Abstract of the United States.*

Where and how is there a bias? Certainly there has been discrimination in employment, housing, and so forth. But specifically, how do blacks suffer discrimination in the criminal justice system? If the factors that militate toward lenient sentence disposition tend to characterize whites more than blacks, the same is true for rich versus poor, old versus young, and female versus male. We can probably never unravel this tangle of human values. Each discovery of bias drives the analysis deeper and deeper into the human psyche and definitions of justice. This doesn't mean that discrimination isn't real and insidious. The Kerner Commission and the Commission on Violence both supply ample evidence of its reality.[4] But it does mean that doing something about it—even if the data were unequivocal—will be very hard.

Length of Sentence. The third "assault" is mounted by those who argue that not only do we imprison too many people, we lock them up for too long. If the ratio of persons subject to corrections in the United States were the same as it is in Sweden, only 150,000 instead of 500,000 persons would be subject to control.[5] Moreover, sentences in the United States are considerably longer in duration:[6]

[T]he following figures give some support to what is an observable difference. *National Prisoner Statistics*, published by the Federal Bureau of Prisons, in 1960 reported that the average time a prisoner served before he was released from a state institution in this country was 2 years and 4 months. Compare this with sentences imposed in Sweden in 1964. In that year 10,535 prisoners were received into Swedish prisons on fixed prison sentences. Their division by duration of sentence was:

Sentence Imposed	Total	% of Total
All Cases	10,535	100.0
Under 2 months	3,208	31.0
2 months to 6 months	3,973	38.0
6 months to 1 year	2,261	21.0
1 year to 2 years	887	8.0
2 years to 4 years	168	1.0
4 years to 10 years	30	0.3
10 years and over	8	0.08

Higher imprisonment rates may reflect a higher crime rate (which in turn reflects social differences between the two countries). Nevertheless, it has yet to be established that imprisoning a larger number of people reduces crime.

Indeterminacy. The fourth attack on sentencing is an attack on the indeterminate sentence. One of the rationales for indeterminacy was that treatment in corrections couldn't work until parole authorities were given the discretion to "hang onto" an offender until the right treatment results had been produced.

But there simply is no evidence that treatment, tied to indeterminacy, has been effective. So as the rehabilitative model is weakened or overridden by new purposes, indeterminacy is correspondingly weakened. And if this is so, in states where the judge is given wide latitude in setting the parameters of indeterminacy, one of the fundamental rationales for such latitude is weakened as well. However, in states like California, where the judge has had little choice but to impose "the term prescribed by law," the abrogation of indeterminacy will thrust discretion back to the judge from the parole board. In fact, California, where indeterminacy has reigned supreme, is now considering repeal of the legislation authorizing the indeterminate sentence.[7]

If indeterminacy is reduced or statutorily eliminated, the length of sentence might be reduced, on the average. This might happen without direct intervention because the indeterminate sentence has caused a discernible statistical drift toward longer sentences,[8] although intentional statutory action also might play a part.[c] There is no evidence that shorter terms in other countries have increased recidivism. (Of course, shorter sentences may reduce the deterrent and incapacitative effects of imprisonment.)

The elimination of indeterminacy also holds implications for correctional programming. With program participation linked to parole decisions, almost all program activities in the prison (or on probation) are tainted with coerciveness. If indeterminacy is reduced or eliminated (coupled as it must be with fixed-term sentences largely matched to the nature of the offense), it may be possible to provide program opportunities that inmates can choose more freely.

Parole. Another assault on sentencing started as an assault on parole. Offenders with substantial interests at stake are given hearings only a few minutes long without the benefit of counsel or confrontation of witnesses against them, and then receive no explanation or rationale for the decision that is rendered. As parole abuses have been documented, some people have argued that parole should be abolished.[9] And one of the reasons advanced for its abolition is that almost all the information pertinent to the determination of the release date for a given offender is available at the time of sentencing.[10] Hence the judiciary has been sloughing its responsibility for tailoring the penalty to the offender to the largely ungoverned and ungovernable parole process. (To some, "sloughing" is the whole idea—the parole board is supposed to do what it does, not the judge.) The court, then, is the proper focus of reform—if the judges do their job, parole might become unnecessary:

Parole allows many actors in the criminal justice system to hide the real nature of their actions and thereby escape responsibility for them. District attorneys may call for and judges may impose excessively long sentences in the name of law and order, knowing that the deferred sentencing process of parole will

---

[c]Other factors influence length of sentences—including increased use of probation instead of incarceration for lesser offenses—but the impact of indeterminacy is substantial.

mitigate their personal harshness. The parole board's extensive and invisible discretion makes it possible for these officials to mislead the public.

The present system encourages partial avoidance of responsibility through the maintenance within itself of a relatively invisible agency that mitigates the harshness of the rest of the system. For example, the legislature can define crimes and harsh penalties without defining sentences or bearing the responsibility of knowing the penalties will be carried out. The prosecutor can prosecute crimes or plea bargain and avoid the moral responsibility of seeking a definite sentence. Judges can convict and avoid imposing penalties. The public sanctions the actions of the professionals in the area, leaving the dirty work to the parole board.[11]

Plea-Bargaining. The trial is no longer the embodiment of due process because it is nearly extinct; plea-bargaining has taken its place. Of the roughly 100,000 misdemeanor defendants in New York City in 1971, over 98,000 pleaded guilty. Accused felons were no more combative—in the first 8 months of 1971, of the 2067 convicted of felonies in the Bronx, 1969 pleaded guilty. The pleas were not entered because the odds against acquittal were insurmountable. During the same 8-month period, 140 defendants went to trial; 42 were acquitted. The chances of acquittal were even greater—about 60 percent—for misdemeanor defendants.[12]

The simple reason why so many defendants plead guilty is that the system forces them to; if more defendants demanded trials, the criminal justice system would disintegrate. The pressures on the prosecution, judge, and defense counsel to maintain the flow of "copped pleas" is so great that the court has become a revolving door for more than just the drunk. Plea-bargaining, then, is a poker game played by people with different degrees of power and little stake in the outcome. It generally takes place hastily in the judge's chambers, often without the defendant present. The defendant's disposition is made by public servants playing with play money.

And the results of plea-bargaining are widely disparate. The poor, who are most often represented by public defenders, rarely receive sentences comparable to those who have economic leverage, private counsel, and social and political affinities. But even more tragically, those who refuse to bargain their lives away and insist on going to trial almost inevitably receive harsher sentences than those who copped pleas; they are punished because they seek to exercise their constitutional rights. There is at least one other argument against plea-bargaining. Ohlin and Remington pointed out some years ago that extensive plea-bargaining gutted attempts to reform sentencing laws and practices. Given the place in plea-bargaining, durable reform of sentencing is less needed because equity can supposedly be served by the judges' wide discretion in shaping the results of the plea bargain.[13]

As a result of these problems and others there has been a movement to abolish, or at least to limit, the use of plea-bargaining. The National Advisory Commission on Criminal Justice Standards and Goals took this position.[14] But plea-bargaining hangs on largely because the alternative—trials for all—is so untenable. Beyond this, there are those who continue to favor it. At a recent national meeting of district attorneys, the conferees unanimously endorsed the practice.[15]

Plea-bargaining affects the correctional system in five ways:

1. It bases sentencing more on the relative bargaining power of the offender and less on the "needs" of the offender or the threat to society.[d]
2. It may spark substantial resentment among prisoners about inequities in the system that may undercut rehabilitation and compound the problems of correctional administrators.
3. It may reduce the "levels" of punishment because most offenders are not sentenced on the basis of the statutory penalties for the offenses they committed, but are generally given a lesser, "discounted" sentence.
4. As a corollary to no. 3, statutory penalties may have to be kept high for the "discounted" penalties to be severe enough. (Although most statutes were not promulgated with a "discount" effect in mind, it can be argued that they have not been reduced because in practice they are largely ignored.)
5. The power of parole boards may be increased. Because the records of inmates contain accounts of their offenses, parole boards may be tempted to appraise the seriousness of the crime on the basis of the "official record" rather than the actual disposition.[16]

There may be a more fundamental issue. Plea-bargaining depends on wide sentencing latitude. If sentencing discretion is reduced or eliminated, both sides to the bargain will have less to work with. This is a concrete example of the systemic interaction of reforms. Plea-bargaining depends on the indeterminate sentence because it gives both the prosecution and the defense some room in which to maneuver. But if the indeterminate sentence disappears, how much room will be left? The prosecution could and probably will increase the number of chargeable offenses, but there is a limit to this sort of escalation.

The Effectiveness of Corrections:
The Evaluation Problem

Another major pressure for reform has been the apparent inability of the rehabilitative model to stand up under scrutiny. What do we really know

---

[d]As Albert W. Alschuler puts it, in "The Prosecutor's Role in Plea Bargaining" (*University of Chicago Law Review* 50 [1968]:112):

> The guilty-plea system does not, in my opinion, merit sweeping condemnation as either too harsh or too generous. It might, however, be described by words that Justice Benjamin N. Cardozo once used in a different context: This method of determining the fate of men accused of crime is "stern often when it should be mild, and mild often when it should be stern." . . . It is as irrational in its mercies as in its rigors.

about the effectiveness of treatment programs and other correctional modalities?

Methodological Considerations. Our first task is to look at corrections in the context of the entire criminal justice system. Too often we think the job of corrections is solely to reduce the likelihood of future criminal behavior by the offender in custody. But as I have pointed out, the correctional system also serves to deter, to render "just deserts," and to incapacitate. Most of the research has looked at only one parameter: the rate of rearrest and reincarceration of exoffenders. Before examining the evidence on treatment, we will look at other correctional modalities in terms of their role in the criminal justice system as a whole. But first a word about "effectiveness."

The major measure of treatment effectiveness is the proportion of those released who are reincarcerated. But there isn't common agreement on a standard measure of recidivism. Should the offender who is reincarcerated on a charge fifteen years after his first arrest be considered a recidivist? If a recidivist, should his reimprisonment be counted along with the four-time loser locked up for the fifth time two months after release? The National Advisory Commission on Criminal Justice Standards and Goals in 1973 proposed a standard national definition of recidivism—a rearrest and conviction or revocation of parole within five years after the latest release. Leaving aside the merits of this definition, the utility of a common definition for at least some research and policy purposes is obvious.

A second issue arises from a consideration of outcomes. What is a good outcome in corrections? Even with a standard definition of recidivism, if within three years X is arrested and convicted of an offense that is at least as serious as his most recent offense, it's clear that that's not a good outcome. But if X reverses the recent trend and becomes an elected official, that probably is a good result. But what if X just disappears and never turns up arrested anywhere? Is that a good outcome? It may be, but we don't know, given that only a fraction of criminal activity is detected. And finally, what if X is rearrested, but on a lesser charge than his previous conviction—has corrections reduced the marginal productivity of his criminal activity and hence produced a good outcome?

Because so much of the fight about crime centers on its effectiveness, a realistic set of measures should be developed. Any such measure or measures should reflect not only rates of rearrest and/or reincarceration within a specified period, (based on a common definition in some cases and, when unwarranted, on special definitions), but also at least two other variables: (1) the relative "success" of those who do not recidivate in terms of employment, social adjustment, and so forth; and (2) a scale weighted for the seriousness of subsequent offenses.

The Relative Effectiveness of Various Correctional Modalities. The tools we have are few: execution, the prison, probation, diversion, and various special dispositions.[e] How effective are they?

---

[e]In rare instances judges will tailor the sentence to the peculiar "needs" of the offender. Normally this occurs only in misdemeanor cases where statutory constraints are absent.

Some criteria are needed. Four measures can be used: (1) the degree to which the tool prevents repetition of criminal behavior; (2) whether the tool reduces the "seriousness" of subsequent crime if detected; (3) both the general and specific deterrent effect of the tool; and (4) how incapacitative is it.

Execution. The point is obvious—except for general deterrence. Until recently, research failed to reveal any deterrent effect. To quote one authority: "Research has shown that homicide rates are unaffected by capital punishment. . . ."[17] But there has been recent evidence that reopens the case. Isaac Ehrlich, in a widely discussed article, argues that the deterrent impact of execution is not only discernible but spectacular: "In fact, the empirical analysis suggests that on the average the tradeoff between the execution of an offender and the lives of potential victims it might have saved was of the order of 1:8 during the years 1933-1967 in the United States."[18] The furor over Ehrlich's research indicates how emotionally and politically charged the issue is. A whole industry of researchers has been loosed to refute it. Yet it is important that we try to resolve it dispassionately. If the evidence shows a deterrent effect, we will have learned something very important about deterrence. This does not mean, however, that we will be compelled to use capital punishment. On the contrary, opposition to it can then proceed along the often incompletely articulated moral lines upon which it is often based.

Probation. Probation can be considered with the prison because there has been some comparative research. Unfortunately, the picture isn't all that clear, although the studies that have been done show that probation seems to work just as well as the prison. For example, in summarizing much of the research, Martinson says that there is "some slight evidence that, at least under some circumstances, probation will make an offender's future chances better than if he had been sent to prison. Or at least, probation may not worsen those chances."[19] And in a review of California programs, the California Youth Authority concluded that "offenders . . . can be *as safely* and at least as effectively handled in intensive intervention programs [probation] without institutionalization." [emphasis added][20]

But there are some problems. First, almost all the research is in terms of the relative effectiveness of probation vis-à-vis imprisonment. Probation may not be less effective, but is it any more effective?

The second problem stems from the difficulty in matching samples of offenders. Offenders who are put on probation are presumably better risks than those who are incarcerated. This has led some, such as Wilson, to conclude that probation isn't necessarily preferable to the prison.[21]

The final problem is that the probation-versus-prison question is usually framed solely in terms of recidivism. There are other tests. For example, it is clear that the maximum security prison is a superb incapacitation device, and hence may be a preferable disposition for some who may be prone to crime even if they would fare as well on probation. And it also would seem, although the evidence is lacking, that imprisonment has a greater deterrent effect, or at least it should if the certainty of imprisonment were as high as that of probation. Finally, there is simply no evidence on seriousness. All we have are crude reconviction rates. But we would learn something if offenders released from probation were reconvicted of less serious offenses than offenders with comparable conviction records who were released from prison.

Diversion.[f] There is one program that is different from probation. In recent years the diversion of alleged offenders has become very popular. A diversion program is any program that officially diverts an alleged offender from the traditional criminal justice system and into a special treatment program in lieu of trial or other disposition. Yet despite its glamor, it may have been oversold. Zimring argues that it is a "healthy" reform but that the zeal about it has outstripped the evidence: "Diversion programs, if designed and executed humanely, are probably a healthy reform in the present state of American criminal justice. As a result of uninformed evaluation efforts, they are also oversold and widely misconceived."[22]

What is the evidence? Nora Klapmuts says that there isn't any: "[T]he effectiveness of diversion really has not been tested."[23] But it has. What Klapmuts must mean is that diversion hasn't adequately been measured against other "correctional" programs; but even then it has. For example, in the prototype program, the Manhattan Court Employment Project, which was begun in 1968, after fourteen months the rearrest rates for participants who successfully completed the program and had their charges dismissed was 15.8 percent; for participants "terminated" from the program it was 30.8 percent; and for the "control" group, it soared to 41.6 percent.[24,g] However, if Klapmuts is referring to long-term recidivism rates, she's right, because diversion programs haven't been around long enough to test.

There are other difficulties. Offenders qualifying for diversion are obviously a rather select group. It is difficult to compare their outcomes with other offenders' outcomes,[h] particularly because of the ethical problems in using

---

[f]Diversion programs will be discussed in more detail in the next chapter.

[g]There are some limitations to this study because the populations were not matched, as Vorenberg and Vorenberg note: "In evaluating these figures, it should be noted that eligibility requirements have varied over the life of the project and that the comparison of those who stayed with the project and those who dropped out is necessarily not on a matched basis." (Vorenberg and Vorenberg, "Early Diversion," p. 161.)

[h]Zimring, in "Measuring the Impact," acknowledges the difficulties in evaluating diversion programs, but finds earlier "evaluations" to be highly misleading; based on a crude matching of diverted and nondiverted offenders, he concludes that diversion has a much more marginal impact on recidivism than generally believed.

matched populations. In addition, diversion is not cheap; it costs about $635 per offender more than the cost of conventional pretrial dispositions.[i]

What about other measures of effectiveness? The answer is simple: No studies have been undertaken. So as with probation, all we can do is speculate. The deterrent effect of diversion is probably low,[25] although it may have a "special" deterrent effect, especially because frequently the "diversionee" is subjected to more social control in the diversion program than if he or she had been conventionally processed. The diversionee, like the probation subject, is not incapacitated as the inmate is, but because diversion is a highly structured program with numerous participant requirements, diversion may be slightly more incapacitative than probation. And, again, we have no data on seriousness.

The lack of information here is particularly troubling. Substantial amounts of time, energy, and resources are being invested in diversion. Yet beyond the descriptive level, we don't know much about it. Diversion has been around long enough now to be something more than an experiment. If this is so, and if it works, then it is hard to justify its lavishness for just a handful of offenders. And if it isn't working, the money being spent on it might very well be better spent elsewhere.

Correctional Treatment Programs. To this point the relative effectiveness of the principal correctional modalities has been the focus. In this section, the question is, "What is the relative effectiveness of those techniques used to correct offenders once the system has got them?" The techniques are many and varied—individual and group counseling, individual psychotherapy, medical treatment, job training, remedial education, and so on.

The principal source of information is Martinson's comprehensive examination of treatment programs.[26] In reviewing studies of effectiveness, he concludes:

[T]hese data, involving over two hundred studies and hundreds of thousands of individuals as they do, are the best available, and give us very little reason to hope that we have in fact found a sure way of reducing recidivism through rehabilitation. This is not to say that we found no instances of success or partial success; it is only to say that these instances have been isolated, producing no clear pattern to indicate the efficacy of any particular method of treatment.[27]

Significantly, though, Martinson is not saying that treatment can't work, but that "it is just possible that some of our treatment programs *are* working to some extent, but our research is so bad that it is incapable of telling." [emphasis in original][28] In fact, there are reported successes in individual

---

[i]See "Pretrial Intervention: A Cost-Benefit Analysis" (full reference, note 34). However, as noted, the total cost through adjudication and correctional disposition makes diversion cheaper.

programs.[j] But in the aggregate, the data amount to nothing more than minor statistical perturbations. Nevertheless, treatment advocates are not yet convinced even though they are maintaining a low profile. There is, in other words, a residual belief in the efficacy of treatment despite the evidence (see pp. 31-35). And this belief might be at least partially sound. What loosed the critics of rehabilitation was the inherently coercive nature of those rehabilitation programs designed to remake offenders into model middle-class citizens—a status most liberal middle-class critics seek desperately to escape. But amidst the horror stories, many genuinely horrific, were some ideas and programs essentially of the employment, skill, artistic and education varieties, which were and are considered to be "rehabilitative," which got smelly when the stink about the behavior alteration programs arose.

The Prison and Its Alternatives

The Fortress Prison

We must destroy the prison, root and branch. That will not solve our problem, but it will be a good beginning.... Let us substitute something. Almost anything will be an improvement. It cannot be worse. It cannot be more brutal and more useless.[29]

Frank Tannenbaum made that statement in 1922, but sympathy for it is as high now as ever. But despite the arguments, nothing seems to be happening. The Federal Bureau's budget for "buildings and facilities" for fiscal year 1975, for example, is $35 million, larger than any other previous year's budget. With this money the bureau plans to build three new institutions. The many groups proposing moratoria on new prison construction should be pleased with their persuasiveness.[k]

---

[j]There is also evidence about "successes" abroad; for example, there are glowing reports about the Hestedvester program. See Georg K. Stürup, *Treating the Untreatable* (Baltimore: Johns Hopkins University Press, 1968). But the chief difficulty is that almost all "successful" treatment programs involve careful selection by the staff of those "suitable" for the program. Thus a spectacularly low recidivism rate of the program's graduates may tell more about its wisdom in selecting "successful" candidates to work with than the ability of the program to transform the human personality. Such skepticism should not obscure the fact that some programs (such as self-help groups, particularly outside of prison) do have an impact on offender behavior—but it must involve a decision on the part of either the offender or the program director, which rules out the use of such programs as massive programs to "treat" or "rehabilitate" offenders.

[k]The construction budgeted for the near future includes $159 million for two new prisons ($79 million), the Butner "Center for Correctional Research" ($15 million), and improvement of existing facilities ($65 million). Four new "metropolitan correctional centers" are budgeted at a total of $40 million. See *The Budget of the U.S. , 1976, Appendix* (Washington, D.C.: U.S. Government Printing Office, 1975), p. 606.

Traditional practices have also continued. This is nowhere more true than in the environment of new prisons. William Nagel, in *The New Red Barn*, describes his impressions:

We did see some imaginative and innovative architecture which tried quite valiantly to make less obvious the fact of confinement. Ornamental grilles and hollow blocks sometimes are used instead of bars. Internal walls are well glazed. Winding paths replace the long bleak corridors. Landscaped lawns and gardens cause some of the uninitiated to complain about "those country clubs for convicts." The grim stone wall is no longer built. The staff of these new facilities, many college trained, hustle at their innumerable, important tasks—supervising, teaching, counseling, training, treating, disciplining.

This sounds good, but read further:

Yet in our conversations with inmates and staff alike and in our observations, we heard and saw the old preoccupation—control. We also observed deep mutual suspicion, great cynicism, and pervasive hypocrisy as the kept and the keepers played old games with each other while using the new sophisticated language of today's behavioral sciences. I have not worked in a prison since 1960, but it was as if everything had changed, yet nothing had changed. The institutions were new and shiny, yet in all their new finery they still seemed to harden everyone in them. Warm people enter the system wanting desperately to change it, but the problems they find are so enormous and the tasks so insurmountable that these warm people turn cold. In time they can no longer allow themselves to feel, to love, to care. To survive, they must become callous. The prison experience is corrosive for those who guard and those who are guarded. This reality is not essentially the product of good or bad architecture. It is the inevitable product of a process that holds troubled people together in a closed and limited space, depriving them of their freedom, their families, and their humanity while expecting a relatively few employees to guard, control, punish, and redeem them.[30]

Finally, it is clear that a "return" to the community requires the prison (or at least most of them) to be located there as well. But has it (or can it) happen? No. As Nagel points out, nearly all of the 23 most recently built correctional facilities are located in sparsely populated areas. Nor is it hard to figure out why. Land costs less in rural areas, and more important, there are fewer people around to object to the location. It seems that the only way a prison can be located in a city is when a once-rural institution is absorbed into a rapidly expanding city (the federal prison at Lompoc, California, 120 miles north of Los Angeles, may soon become a community-correctional facility in Los Angeles).

The real barrier to getting rid of the prison is that we don't know what to substitute.

Community-Based Corrections

What do we use to handle those we remove from their cells? The answer most frequently given is corrections in the community. But this concept lacks content. Most of the literature on the subject is descriptive rather than analytic and seems to place community-based corrections on a rough continuum with progenitor programs, such as the halfway house. The literature is short on analysis because only infrequently are the tough questions asked: Whose community? What inmates? How is security ensured? But despite the lack of answers the community reform movement is flourishing, even if only a few now enjoy its fruits. As Edward Eldefonso says,

Disenchantment with imprisonment as a corrective measure seems to have led to a less than critical acceptance of noninstitutional alternatives as "more effective." Both classification and evaluation of community correctional programs are complicated by this lack of clarity and by the interference of value-laden assumptions.[31]

It is probably true that neither the goals of treatment nor simple isolation are well served in the fortress prison. Many argue that treatment simply won't work in a warehouse. And isolation in rural America, monitored by guards with alien social and cultural backgrounds, may be too severe a punishment for contemporary sensibilities. It also may be true that many offenders recidivate because the social and family links that could sustain them upon release have been shattered by their forcible removal. But even with these givens, no set of specifications for corrections naturally follows, save its locus in some community chosen for its habitability for the selected offender. If this is so, then where are the good programs, and what has their impact been?

One of the arguments about why we don't know much about community-based corrections—and in turn don't entirely trust the decarcerationists—is that there isn't much to look at. Some argue that community-based corrections hasn't really been tried. But until it is, and until we know something about its relative efficacy, decarceration will be slowed if not stopped.

But the argument that community-based corrections hasn't been tried is ultimately specious. Probation is a community-based program. True, when we hear the phrase "community-based corrections," we tend to think of something other than probation, in part because we think of the community in this sense as a substitute for the prison and hence appropriate for offenders for whom probation has been considered and rejected. Also, we envision a richer, more complete "package" of programs and services in community-based corrections than we have ever provided in probation. The community affords a greater variety of program opportunities and, at least in some cases—like the half-way house—more security to the community than probation. But this is all a matter of degree. The site is the same—the community, presumably from whence the offender came—the purpose is the same—to "correct." And the technology is essentially the same, although we seem prepared to experiment with more elaborate tools in the new community corrections movement.

There are other similarities. One of the reasons we are considering the community as the optimal site for corrections is that we recognize that for the majority of offenders, *including* many who are now locked up, the community is a better place to try to do the job. The evidence supporting the efficacy of probation, although somewhat mixed, aids the case. Hence the argument that community-based corrections is somehow different from probation because "different" offenders would be involved largely fails. This is so because if we imprison too many, those we mistakenly incarcerate would fare no worse on probation, and accordingly, there should be no discernible increase in the crime rates with its underuse.

Moreover, do we really mean to depart radically from the probation model when we design community-based correctional programs? Most of the rehabilitative technology we might think about installing in the new community-based programs has been convincingly repudiated by recent research on the prison and on the experimental probation programs. There have been no treatment breakthroughs that warrant the assumption that new programs can be devised in the community that will be much different from those we have already tried. Finally, the resources simply might not be there. The Federal Bureau and many of the states fervently endorse community-based corrections and then fatten their budgets for new prisons.[32]

All that has happened is a conceptual breakthrough—a relatively new way of thinking about the proper site for the correction of most offenders. In the past the prison was presumed to be the proper place for corrections unless the judge and the prosecutor could be convinced otherwise. In the future the presumption will probably lie against the prison, except for the most hardened few. But in practice, corrections will look much the same. It's fine to tout something new like community-based corrections. Maybe the catchwords will instill a new dedication to humanizing the correctional process. But to be realistic, at the program level, community-based corrections is a fundamental extension of probation,[1] and there's nothing wrong with that.

Diversion

There is a familiar litany in the literature:[33] Diversion is premised on the need to reduce the "penetration" of the offender into the system in order to enhance the prospects of rehabilitation; selection criteria are often arbitrary; in effect, the participant is deprived of the opportunity to prove his or her innocence; the program is "coercive"; diversion does not reduce overall system costs because it

---

[1]Community-based corrections can be different in practice than probation, principally in its richness and variety. There is one specific way that community-based corrections might depart significantly from probation. Rather than trying to erect new programs that differ only slightly from probation, the "private" sector might be used imaginatively. There are such cases—Synanon, Delancey Street, the Fortune Society, and so forth. In the absence of community, offenders might be given the opportunity to create the communities they either never have had or from which they were irreversibly wrenched when incarcerated. A voucher system might even be developed. There are resources in most communities that could be perceptively assembled to give this approach a try.

is expensive and because there is no hard evidence that recidivism is reduced; and diversion may result in greater, not lesser, social control—first, because diversion programs are simply more subtle social control systems, and second, because there is some evidence that the "places" within the traditional system otherwise occupied by diversionees are taken by others.

Diversion is philosophically consistent with rehabilitative theory.[m] For example, diversion makes it possible to experiment with some rehabilitative technology that is not normally available in the prison. Program expenditures for diversion are considerably higher than in traditional dispositions: $695 per capita on the average, versus $360.[34] (Ultimate pre- and post-disposition costs are reversed, however; $695 for diversion and $875 for traditional dispositions.)[35] So more money is available to deploy treatment techniques. In addition, diversion programs frequently can escape civil service requirements and other limitations. In short, diversion is the rehabilitator's dream—nearly all the things which supposedly compromise rehabilitation in the prison (or on the streets) can be avoided with diversion. But of course these obvious advantages may be offset by the movement away from rehabilitation theory. Because diversion is so much in the rehabilitation camp, if rehabilitation itself is gutted and replaced with new objectives—such as retribution and deterrence—its future may be clouded. In the past few years it has been a glamour stock, but with the overall decline in the value of rehabilitation, the bottom might drop out.

If diversion is just a fad, it will have little if any future impact on corrections. But if it remains a feature of criminal justice practice, what are some of the implications for correctional practice?

First, diversion is a correctional program although its origins may be different. There is no final adjudication of guilt in most cases; but nevertheless, the participant in diversion is there because of a "disposition" and, accordingly, he or she must participate to the satisfaction of the program personnel, whose function is similar to a parole board's. Also, a loss of freedom is entailed as much and often more as in the case of probation—program requirements are substantial. Finally, there is evidence that diversion programs, as they become more widespread, are slowly succumbing to institutional controls exercised by the traditional criminal justice system. This has been the fate of the progenitor program—the Manhattan Court Employment project—and it may happen to other programs as well.[36] Hence, if diversion remains on the scene and even expands, the map of corrections is bound to change because a new form of corrections will have emerged along with imprisonment, probation, and parole.

Just because diversion may be absorbed into corrections eventually doesn't mean that it won't affect the correctional system in the interim. First, to the extent that diversion skims off the most likely to succeed, conventional

---

[m]One way it is not consistent lies in its intent to minimize offender penetration into the correctional system.

corrections is left with a more intractable residue. Second, if resources are scarce (and when aren't they?), the comparative richness of diversion programs may result in even greater starvation for the remainder of corrections,[n] particularly if diversion remains the darling of legislators, private foundations, and federal agencies.

There may be some positive consequences. If rehabilitation retains some utility in corrections, the most successful rehabilitative elements in diversion might fertilize conventional correctional programs. And finally, because diversion is one of the few new community-based correctional programs, it might yield some valuable advice on the construction of other such programs if the shift to the community in correctional practice continues.

It has also been argued that diversion may diminish the caseload for corrections by diminishing the number of persons processed in the traditional system. The argument is doubtful, however. The evidence is that diversion does not diminish the caseload but only alters its composition, or if diversion does skim off some who might end up in prison, then those empty cells are filled up by other offenders who don't qualify for diversion.[37] Hence it is likely that the same number of offenders will be processed in the traditional system as before, but that they will be more difficult to handle.

On balance it is doubtful that the "successes" of diversion will make the job of corrections any easier.

The Implications of a "Shift" to the Community

Some serious questions remain when we turn to the potential effects of a shift to the community. The release of more offenders to the community, whatever the programs are called, invariably will diminish the system's incapacitative capability. And if those who argue that most crime is committed by a small number of recycled crooks are correct, unless we can keep them all locked up, we should see a rise in the crime rate. Perhaps new sophisticated surveillance techniques might be used to offset losses in security, but many such techniques run afoul of well-established constitutional and legal principles that won't be bent easily.

The deterrent power of corrections also may suffer unless we find the means to make the community-based correctional experience as patently harsh as the prison. It is certainly possible to do so, but at least in the short run the community is going to look like a picnic compared to the prison, both to the offender and to the general public.

There is no way of knowing what will happen to recidivism. Probation has

---

[n]Of course, if diversionees don't recidivate, their part in diversion may be cost-effective; although diversion is more expensive than other pretrial dispositions, it is cheaper in the long run because incarceration or lengthy probation may be avoided.

been shown to be at least as effective as the prison, but with the influx of offenders who heretofore would have been incarcerated, the odds may shift. All we can say is that the system can be monitored. Programs of evaluation should be set up quickly to watch the results.

The Nature of Correctional Facilities:
A Possible Future

The first issue is size. European experience is always mentioned in discussions of size. Because the average size of European penal institutions, particularly those in Scandinavia and the Netherlands, is smaller on the average than the size of U.S. penal institutions, smallness is assumed to be better. We are told, for example, that ". . . experts are uniformly convinced that 'fortress' prisons are an unmitigated contamination of criminal justice."[38] But the evidence is shaky. There are some glowing reports: Norval Morris has reported some anecdotal "successes,"[39] but there is also some evidence that recidivism rates are no better, on the average, than they are here.

What are the advantages of smallness? Because we have little if any evidence to argue for smallness on its own merits, the advantages are all largely presumed. Security should be easier; specialized treatment should be easier; and with more small institutions, it should be easier to place inmates according to need. Moreover, violence in the prison might be controlled more easily, and the correctional experience might be "humanized" more readily. These are valid objectives, but there are at least two problems. First, to the extent that we move away from the individualized treatment model in corrections, the advantages of the small institution regarding individual treatment are vitiated. Second, we simply don't have enough of them to test. Perhaps we will in the future, but one thing is clear—to test the small institution, we will still have to go into rural areas to do so. There isn't much evidence that prisons are being built anywhere else.

Ultimately, the question of size is linked with the questions of location and purpose. If, contrary to the evidence available today, future prisons are located closer to major urban centers, they will have to be smaller facilities because of land costs and citizen opposition. Resources and public opinion, not the ideological preferences of reformers, will influence this decision. Second, if the prison is reconceptualized in concert with other reforms within the correctional system—particularly the proposal that only the truly dangerous require incarceration—a smaller institution may result. A smaller facility also would be more suited to short-term "shock" incarceration that has been proposed recently. The idea is that many offenders, not just the dangerous, might be "stung" by a brief exposure to imprisonment, even if they wouldn't qualify under conventional sentencing practices otherwise. Because the shock wouldn't last very long—two to four weeks or so—large, well-furbished institutions wouldn't be required.[40]

("Shock probation"—a short period of incarceration followed by traditional probation—has also been proposed.)

If the prison of the future is thought of as having essentially two purposes— the long-term incarceration of the dangerous offender and the short-term "shock" treatment of many others who are not deemed as dangerous—a large facility isn't needed. Presumably, too, there won't be that many so-called dangerous offenders, so the number of beds needed will be far fewer—although there is no reason to assume that the beds will be any closer to the city. The dangerous won't be targets for rehabilitation anyway, and many citizens will be alarmed by the prospect of rapists and murderers bedding down around the corner.

For other offenders, most of them involved in community-based programs, small prisonlike structures may still be needed near or in the urban areas to serve as "outpatient" facilities with a few beds for acute, short-term cases. It may not be appropriate to call such facilities prisons, but if they serve to incapacitate offenders, even if only for a few hours or days, the term will suffice.

Another word about function. If the reform movements are as strong as they appear to be (despite their current lack of coherence), a new blueprint for the prison of the future may emerge. And if that blueprint is based on a new set of functions for the prison, what might happen? There are three possible new functions: the long-term incarceration of the dangerous offender; the short-term "shock" treatment of some other offenders; and the use of a community facility designed more for support than for isolation or incapacitation. The first purpose, and the facilities to match it, has been discussed already. So has the second—but I should mention that the working assumption for it is that community-based correctional programs will need a backstop—a place other than the prison for the dangerous, where offenders, committing mild infractions, can be placed while they continue to participate in community-based correctional programs.

The third facility must be linked with community correctional programming, which will be discussed on pp. 98-100. The fundamental rationale is that most offenders released to the community have no communities to go to. Too often we assume that everyone has a home, but this may not be the case for many offenders—and even if it is, that home may not be conducive to staying straight. Hence what may be needed is a kind of community center—similar to some halfway houses except that no one will bed down there and there will be no locks and bars—for offenders participating in diversion programs and new community correctional programs, to be used for group meetings, recreation, counseling, administration, and so on.

Related Issues in Correctional Practice

The most important issues facing corrections today are the criticisms directed toward it and the future of the prison. But there are other related issues that will shape the subtle character of whatever system emerges in the future. In this section we will examine some of these questions.

Correctional Programs

Unless we return to a prison system where we lock people up, throw away the key, and slide gruel under the door, the prison will have to have a "program." It may be minimal—perhaps nothing more than an exercise yard and a chaplain—or it may be ambitious and ample, including formal educational opportunities and individual psychotherapy. But whatever the program, there are three central questions: whether the program is treatment-oriented, whether participation is voluntary, and whether participation is linked to early release.

Treatment. Treatment is provided if it is assumed that the offender is sick. Then, following the medical model that has been so widespread in corrections in recent years, a program is devised to "cure" him or her. In practice, of course, rarely have programs been designed for the peculiar needs of individual offenders. Instead, group therapy and counseling programs have been used, occasionally coupled with remedial education and job-training opportunities, all forms of rehabilitation, even though some are not therapeutic in nature. It is this treatment or "curative" aspect of rehabilitation, that has been so vigorously attacked—but not because it might not have benefited some individuals, or that it was maliciously conceived. Rather, it has been attacked because there is no evidence that it reduces recidivism, in general, and because "successful" participation in therapeutic programs has been linked to release on parole, and as such has led to serious abuses. But to reject application of the medical model is not the same as rejecting rehabilitation as a purpose for corrections. When rehabilitation is rejected as a purpose, do educational programs go; remedial programs; job training; voluntary group sessions; group therapy sessions? The line between treatment and nontreatment is fuzzy—in fact, it may be impossible to draw. Arguably, then, programs might be judged not on their "treatment" orientation, but on their degree of coerciveness. This is essentially Norval Morris's argument when he proposes "facilitative treatment,"[41] and it is thematically consistent with those who favor "reintegration" as a dominant purpose of corrections as a replacement for rehabilitation.

"Dangerousness" and Prediction. This is one of the key issues in corrections today because the so-called "dangerous" offender presumably contributes disproportionately to the crime rate, and may contribute to the rates of violent crime even more disproportionately. It is also a key issue because its resolution would free other issues for resolution that have been held hostage to it. For example, the widely heralded move to the community has been stymied, at least in part, by our lack of knowledge about who should and should not be candidates for the community.

Yet for all its importance, the issue hasn't been well framed. Is the dangerous offender a "habitual" crook, regardless of the nature of his or her crimes, or merely one who manifests dangerousness in a single crime or only episodically? Also, is dangerousness predicated on bodily harm, or is the recidivating property thief dangerous as well? Finally, is the dangerous offender somehow different from other offenders, biologically or otherwise, or is dangerousness just a matter of degree? The literature isn't very clear on these points. There are a few definitions, particularly statutes authorizing preventive confinement. Maryland has one of the most draconian statutes; it defines a "defective delinquent" (a felicitous term) as an individual who

... by the demonstration of persistent aggravated antisocial or criminal behavior, evidences a propensity toward criminal activity ... as to clearly demonstrate an actual danger to society so as to require such confinement and treatment, when appropriate, as may make it reasonably safe for society to terminate the confinement and treatment.[42]

In the absence of definitional clarity, assume that a dangerous offender is one who engages in destructive behavior either to a person or to property, frequently enough to exhibit a pattern of conduct. Of course, there are a few problems with this formulation. The seemingly equal stress on offenses against the person and to property may offend someone's sense of proportion. To some, no amount of property is worth protecting, but others might prefer to be brutally beaten rather than give up their American Express cards. Depending on the sensibilities of the statute writers, then, the line beyond which a mere offender is transformed into a dangerous offender can be set differently for crimes of violence or of property, whatever seems appropriate.

A second or obvious problem is defining the word "pattern." Should it encompass both the offender who commits a violent assault and has a history of plucking the legs off bugs, and the burglar just caught for the eleventh time? I don't know, but I'm happier applying the term to the latter rather than to the former, for reasons stated below. In any event, accepting the formulation as a working definition, what we do next seems to be predicated on the answers to four fundamental questions:

1. Should someone defined as "dangerous" be detained on a preventive basis, or only on the basis of culpability?
2. Are predictive technologies accurate enough to "legitimate" detention on the basis of dangerousness?
3. What degree of culpability for what type of "predicted" offenses is necessary to treat an offender as dangerous?
4. Once an offender is classified as dangerous, what should the correctional disposition be?

These are all thorny problems, well beyond full discussion here. But the pivotal issue, it seems to me, is whether so-called dangerous offenders should be so classified on the basis of a "prediction" of future socially harmful behavior, or only on the basis of past offenses. This distinction is not made often enough. Frequently, discussions of dangerousness turn quickly and almost exclusively to debates about prediction. If, on the other hand, the offender is to be treated as dangerous solely on the basis of past offenses, there is no need to indulge in debates about prediction—and "indulging" appears to be an accurate term, given the problems of prediction.

A second problem is justification. The criminological literature is filled with discussions of the "justification" for state intervention and control. To some, the justification resides in the very existence of the state and no further discussion is needed. To others at the other end of the pole, the state, because it is morally corrupt, lacks any justification for punishment. But to those who see more subtlety in the question, the problem lies in justifying various differentiations in punishment.

The burglar just arrested for the eleventh time and the burglar just caught for the first time may have committed the same crime, but some justification for differential treatment exists. But what if both burglars were arrested for the first time, burglar A is only eighteen, has a starving mother and six siblings, and is impressively contrite, whereas burglar B is forty-two, single, and unrepentant? If A gets off with a lesser sentence, what is the justification? This, of course, is the potential pitfall of the "just deserts" rationale for sentencing. It can be easily compromised by mitigation. Closer to home, what is the justification for a harsher sentence for burglar C—who has committed an eleventh offense—and a disproportionately lenient disposition for burglar D—who, otherwise similarly situated, has committed a tenth offense? Is labeling burglar C "dangerous" sufficient justification for the more severe sentence?

A third observation concerns prediction. The evidence (some of it discussed on pp. 108-109) strongly suggests that prediction is far from a well-honed instrument. Our criminal justice system is premised, at least in part, on waiting—waiting until someone does something that allows us to intervene. Of course, this is a clumsy way to control crime. As a result, proposals have been made to increase the efficiency of social control by intervening earlier—preferably before something happens. To a limited extent, this has always been done. Police don't sit in their stations waiting for the phone to ring—many are active and visible as a means of deterring criminal activity. They also anticipate crime by being on the spot. And further, there are some borderline cases where police intervene on various pretexts to keep some would-be crooks off-guard. But only in a few instances have we allowed law enforcement officials to detain someone just because he or she might commit a crime. The preventive detention program in Washington, D.C., comes close, but it is conceptually distinguishable because the detainee is already in custody as a result of past behavior. Nevertheless, because of the mounting tide of crime, and "fear in the streets," many would like to fashion a more aggressive law enforcement system. An essential cornerstone of such a system is "prediction." If it can be predicted that A may do B or that X is predisposed to Y, or that R, based on a past record, will invariably do S, then, the argument goes, Why not intervene earlier, either to detain or to "treat" A, X, or R? The same can and has been said about offenders already in custody who might be classified as dangerous.

An enormous amount of effort has been expended to improve predictive techniques, in part because we already rely on prediction in parole determinations and to some extent in judicial sentencing. But how good are these techniques? Norval Morris devotes some time to the question. He reflects on some of the research and the accuracy of prediction:

Two recent studies from the California Department of Corrections Research Group . . . should give pause to any member of a parole board who has confidence in his capacity as a seer of future violent crime. The effort by this skilled research group to develop a "violence prediction scale" for use in parole decisions resulted in 86% of those identified as potentially dangerous failing to commit a violent act (more accurately, failing to be detected in a violent act) while on parole. A parallel effort to predict Youth Authority wards likely to be violent on parole led to no better predictor than a history of actual violence, and that produced a 95% overprediction of violence.[43]

The research support for prediction isn't resounding. Yet the idea persists that somehow we can define dangerousness and then predict its onset. For example, the Standards and Goals Commission includes among its recommendations that "State penal code revisions . . . include a provision that the maximum sentence for any offender *not specifically found to represent a substantial danger* should not exceed five years for felonies other than murder." [emphasis added][44] The intent is sound: Let's not stick people away if we don't have to. But the "intent" cuts both ways. Why not detain those who do represent "a substantial danger"? By whom and how will the determination be made that someone is or is not dangerous? The moral issues and dilemmas we face can best be articulated by quoting again from Morris at some length:

Let us suppose that we have to predict future violence to the person from among one hundred convicted criminals, and let me invent figures that are far superior to anything we can now achieve in practice. Assume that of the one hundred, we select thirty as likely future violent criminals. Despite our prediction of danger, all one hundred are either released or left at large. Their subsequent careers are then followed, and with hypothetical precision we know the results. Of the thirty we predicted as dangerous, twenty did commit serious crimes of violence and ten did not. Of the seventy we declared to be relatively safe, five did commit crimes of physical violence and sixty-five did not.

Prediction		Result	
		No Violent Crime	Violent Crime
Safe	70	65	5
Violent Crime	30	10	20
Total	100	75	25

Reading [the table] one might claim, "We had 80 percent success in our prediction, successfully preselecting twenty out of the twenty-five who later committed serious crimes of violence." Not bad. Of course, we failed to select five of the one hundred who later proved to be dangerous, but that seems a minor failure compared with the twenty serious crimes we could have prevented. Note, however, that we also failed in another way. We selected ten as dangerous—as likely to commit crimes of violence—but they did not. Had we imprisoned the thirty that we predicted as dangerous, in ten cases we would have failed in our prediction by needlessly detaining them. Put more succinctly, we made twenty true positive predictions of violence and ten false positive predictions.

To increase our claimed 80 percent success—to diminish the number of those we predicted as safe but who turned out to be dangerous—we could certainly increase the number of our true positive predictions of dangerousness, but only at the cost of substantially increasing the number of false positive predictions of dangerousness. There, if you will reflect on it, is the moral dilemma we face: how many false positives can be justified for the sake of preventing crime by the true positives?[4] [5]

As refractory as the issue is, it still seems highly suited to policy resolution by state and federal authorities. In other words, if some offenders are to be detained as dangerous, the technology appears to be there to allow legislators to assess the costs and benefits of such a program by "counting" false positives in a way rarely available in most social problem areas. (Such an assessment, of course, would be easier with property-related offenses, which, because they are more frequent, are more predictable.) This isn't an argument for or against the use of predictive technology, just an argument that it might be assessed more rationally than many other technologies because the chips that will fall are very predictable, even if violent offenders aren't.

Because the issue of the dangerous offender has become so prominent and is so central to many of the pending reforms, soon we will be forced to decide whether to try to decide who is and who is not dangerous. Of course, if we choose to try, it doesn't mean that we will have to rely on predictive techniques. We could simply classify as dangerous all offenders who commit more than a certain number of offenses. How this issue will be resolved is unknown—but it is a big issue.

A final observation is that there has been so much prating about the prediction issue that little attention has been given to what we would do with dangerous offenders if we *could* identify them.[46] There are vague references to maximum security prisons for the criminally dangerous, but little specification has emerged beyond that. Will appreciably longer terms be set for the dangerous, even if the instant offense calls for a sentence of considerably less duration? What kind of early release opportunities would exist, if any? And what kind of programs would be made available? These questions haven't been answered and may not be because of all the furor spent over the classification question—perhaps appropriately so.

Coercion and Choice. The following letter from a prisoner was read in hearings before the House Committee on the Judiciary in 1971:

I was recently released from "solitary confinement" after being held therein for 37 months. The silent system was imposed upon me and to even whisper to the man in the next cell resulted in being beaten by guards, sprayed with chemical mace, blackjacked, stomped, and thrown into a strip-cell naked to sleep on a concrete floor without bedding, covering, wash basin, or even a toilet. The floor served as toilet and bed, and even there the silent system was enforced. To let a moan escape your lips because of the pain and discomfort resulted in another beating. I spent not days, but months there during my 37 months in solitary. I have filed every writ possible against the administrative acts of brutality. The State courts have all denied the petitions. Because of my refusal to let the "things die down" and "forget" all that happened during my 37 months in solitary, I am the most hated prisoner in ——— penitentiary, and called a "hard-core incorrigible."

. . . [M]aybe I am an incorrigible, but, if true, it is because I would rather die than to accept being treated as less than a human being. I have never complained of my prison sentence as being unjustified except through legal means of appeals. I have never put a knife on a guard's throat and demanded my release. I know that thieves must be punished and I don't justify stealing, even though I am a thief myself. But now I don't think I will be a thief when I am released. No, I'm not rehabilitated. It's just that I no longer think of becoming wealthy by stealing. I now only think of "killing."

Killing those who have beaten me and treated me as if I were a dog. I hope and pray for the sake of my own soul and future life of freedom that I am able to overcome the bitterness and hatred which eats daily at my soul, but I know to overcome it will not be easy.[47]

The minimization of coercion is the objective of the proponents of reintegration. They desire to rehabilitate, but they know that rehabilitation is out of favor. But most of them also recognize that rehabilitation in a coercive context may be severely compromised. Hence they seek to create a therapeutic climate with a minimum of coercion. In part this is true because they believe, unlike the rigorous behavioral engineer, that inmates must make real choices in prison if they are to make real choices after their release.

Prison normally lacks all that is most valuable to a man—love, loyalty, manly pride. First the man is forced to conform, and soon he finds it easier to let others make his decisions than to make them himself. A man's skills atrophy, and his interests narrow to one or two undemanding pastimes like watching TV, playing cards, or reading novels. Life loses its wonder. Some men shuffle along as if they were trying to hide holes in their shoes.[48]

Prison drastically reduces the number and quality of decisions for the inmate. Prison life is routine and regimented—the "real" decisions are often rebellious. Yet nearly all inmates are returned to free society, and because of their incarceration, are rarely equipped to make decisions after their release. There are some decisions in the prison—whether to join a cultural group or an encounter group, and whether to learn how to paint, or even to read. These are not necessarily insignificant choices, but because they arise in an artificial setting, inmates often perceive them as artificial decisions.

How realistic is a noncoercive corrections, and similarly, how feasible are "real" choices? As long as an offender is subject to restraints that the average citizen is not, and as long as those restraints can be enforced, coercion is present. To be sure, restraints can be relaxed. The prison experience can be made more dignified—the inmate can be relieved of the need to grovel. Outside the prison, work release, for example, affords the inmate an escape from the immediacy of restraint when he or she is on the job. And, of course, probation, given the heavy caseloads carried by probation officers, yields a substantial measure of conditional freedom. But restraints are still present and enforceable. The probationer who fails to keep an appointment can be retrieved and tossed back into the institution.

The community-based correctional movement is premised, in part, on enhancing and expanding offender choice. But will it? If it expands, more offenders will be relocated in the "community" in programs that should offer the inmate more options and more social interaction. But physical security will be less tight in a halfway house, or when some inmates are tiptoeing around the city on furloughs. This is why the crunch may come. If the community is to accept community-based corrections, security must not be greatly relaxed, or at least it must not appear to have been greatly relaxed. To compensate for the inevitable diminution of traditional security—lockups, guards, walls, shake-downs, and so forth—new measures may have to be developed. They are likely to be more sophisticated surveillance techniques. And under these circumstances, coercion may reenter in more subtle forms, and "real" choices may become illusory.

Yet it is undoubtedly true that corrections can be made less overtly coercive. There's no reason why a range of choices can't be made available, and further, no reason why prisoners can't be allowed to pick and choose among them, or not to choose at all. Moreover, there is a clear difference between inmate participation in a job-training program and compulsory inmate participation in a behavioral modification program. The dilution of coercion does not require the dissolution of academic and vocational training opportunities. The major difficulty has been and remains the relationship between program participation, "voluntary" or not, and early release.

Coercion and Parole.

[T] he day the parole board arrives at a prison is a special day. Inmates scheduled to appear before it have looked forward to it for months. They have thought for months about what it takes to get paroled, and most likely have guided their behavior during that time by what they thought would please the board. Individual inmates have or have not participated in prison programs such as vocational training, education or group therapy depending on what they thought the parole board would think of the program.[49]

Shattering this link—the link between program participation and release on parole—is the key to "voluntary" correctional programming. Participation never will be wholly voluntary as long as prison supervisory personnel would rather have an inmate participate than not. But if it can be clearly communicated to the inmate that participation in any or none of the available programs has no direct bearing on release, and if effective and durable safeguards can be introduced, coercion could be reduced significantly. And it can be reduced, perhaps more easily, if the indeterminate sentence is abolished or greatly modified.

A number of proposals—ranging from abolition to modest tinkering—have been made to reform the parole process. Those who argue for abolition do so because of the abuses, but also because they think parole would be unnecessary if the judiciary did its job. Other proposals would retain parole, but subject to guidelines and expanded prisoner protections. For example, a major modification of parole practices has already been implemented in the federal prison system, based on the work of Don M. Gottfredson, et al.[50] The new scheme is based on the use of a set of "salient factors" that ostensibly are related to the risks of further criminal activity. Other proposals usually include widespread inmate protection against abuses of discretion in parole decision-making by introducing some minimal due process protections.

Contracting. Contracting is a recent program innovation that cuts across these issues. It is based on three premises: (1) that a "contract" between inmates and correctional authorities would lend some badly needed substance to parole decision-making; (2) that "tyranny" in the prison might be reduced if the relations between inmates and their keepers were somewhat routinized; and (3) that inmates lack opportunities to make real choices.[51]

A contract, as it is conceived in correctional practice, consists of an agreement between the inmate, correctional authorities, and the parole board. Essentially, it is a promise by the inmate to complete a "treatment" program and to refrain from activities that would subject him or her to discipline. The correctional authorities promise to provide the appropriate training and counseling. The parole board, presumably because there is some "consideration" between it and the inmate, promises to release the inmate when the program has been completed satisfactorily. In theory, then, contracting should replace or reduce indeterminacy, create an atmosphere in which mild behavior modification can occur, and finally, yield some decision-making authority to the inmate and in turn reward the inmate for assuming initiative and responsibility.

The contracting approach is heavily premised on rehabilitative thinking. It is assumed that a workable treatment program can be devised and agreed to by the inmate and correctional authorities. The only major difference is that the inmate participates in constructing the contract and assumes the responsibility for completing it successfully. Contracting is appealing because it fits well with other reform movements—including the "justice model"—and because it gives the inmate more responsibility. But there are some difficulties.

First, the relative bargaining positions of the parties are far from equal.[52] As a practical matter, all that may occur is that the inmate is given a laundry list of program opporunities at the point of incarceration—not unlike what is done now—and told that he or she must agree to one or more of them. Presumably no contract would exist if the inmate didn't want to pursue any program. Moreover, the inmate's participation is closely monitored to help the parole board determine how "successfully" the program is being completed. This mirrors the current situation, in which an inmate's program participation, absent a contract, is often germane to parole. The result may be that a small measure of decision-making is turned over to the inmate, but as a practical matter the amount of real choice the inmate possesses remains very small.

Another major objection to contracting is that it is so squarely premised on rehabilitation, which is fast disappearing in correctional practice. It is presumed that "treatment" will work if the inmate agrees to it in advance. There is no evidence to support this argument, but contracting hasn't been used long enough to determine its long-term effectiveness. Essentially, then, contracting can be thought of as an attempt to superimpose a "legal" or "justice" model on top of the existing medical model to reduce the abuses committed in the name of that model in past practice. The fundamental question, of course, is whether the justice model, even in this limited application, can take root in the anarchy of the modern prison.

Restitution and Victim Compensation. A final method of enhancing the offender's assumption of responsibility has been around for awhile but is now enjoying a revival. Restitution is also premised on a "contract," this time between the offender and the victim for restitution of the loss inflicted by the offender. Basically, the argument is, given the untoward effects of imprisonment, restitution is a simple, easily administered penalty that has been shown to possess a deterrent effect.[53] But again there are some problems. First, a restitution contract presupposes a willing victim. Hence to the extent that victims are unwilling to negotiate, restitution in its traditional form remains a limited tool. On the other hand, restitution arrangements might be explored that require the offender to pay into a common fund that is available generally for victim compensation.

A second problem is that restitution, whether paid directly to the victim or into a fund, represents a "tax" on the offender's legitimate activity after release. Most offenders are released with only pin money. Thereafter, particularly in times of strained economic conditions, exoffenders are greatly disadvantaged in the labor market. If restitution is then required, inevitably it will bite into whatever income the exoffender manages to generate. And this in turn creates a disincentive, or tax, to the offender's legitimate productivity.

Restitution has always lingered on the scene in corrections, but it has received more attention lately as the victim has become more prominent in criminological thinking. The rehabilitative emphasis on the individual offender has resulted in a lack of attention to the victim. But as retributive and deterrent principles reemerge, the emphasis is once again returning to the social order, and concomitantly to the victim's role as a part of that social order. This enlarged interest has taken many forms: victim surveys that attempt to improve the reliability of crime incidence data; research that investigates the texture of the relationship between the victim and the perpetrator; and finally, schemes (some of which have already been implemented) for victim compensation.[54] In part, the reawakening interest in the victim stems from the futility that many have experienced in corrections. If somehow punishment, in any form, could be said to work, less pressure would exist for compensatory treatment of the victim. If society could somehow be "sated" in its punitiveness by seeing its results—pain, deterrence, rehabilitation, and so on—the victim might recede in importance. But this may not be desirable. Leaving aside the public's satisfaction with its punitive efforts, the victim has been ignored far too long. Whenever the victim has no complicity in the offense, there is no reason why society could not fashion compensatory programs to aid those who suffer irreparable harm. This need not be done in derogation of offender due process protections. The two are not mutually contradictory.

Prisoners' Rights. For a long time prisoners had essentially no rights. But in recent years there has been a rush of prisoners' rights litigation and inmate activity. There have been a few animating premises. The first is protection against abuses of discretion. Because many correctional decisions so directly affect the offender's well-being, attempts have been made to introduce as many due process safeguards as possible. A second premise springs from the recognition that offenders rarely make decisions for themselves and that there might be merit in offering them some opportunity to do so, so that when they are released their decision-making capacity hasn't entirely atrophied. One exinmate, now a correctional official, explains:

A man comes home to a few kids and a wife and he's expected to be a provider. He's not been prepared during incarceration to shoulder responsibility. I don't condemn a man who's been out six months and then commits another crime. By returning to prison, he doesn't have to worry . . . .[55]

Prisoners' rights activity is focused on discretion exercised before the accused becomes an offender, while the offender is an offender, and after release, unless release is unconditional. Our focus is on what happens during confinement or on probation and after release. The major discretion points that are under scrutiny are disciplinary actions; exercise of inmate rights, including assembly and speech; transfers while in confinement; parole decisions; and revocation of probation or parole. Full discussion of these issues is more than can be taken on here, but again a couple of observations.

Each of the observations assumes that the way inmates are treated during confinement may have something to do with their behavior after release.

Most inmates perceive the conditions of their confinement as lawless. They are told they have no rights—or at best, just a few privileges—and their experience generally confirms what they are told. As noted earlier, the prison affords few opportunities for real choice. The same can be said about probation, but the number, if not necessarily the quality, of choices is at least greater with probation. However, when offenders are released back to the street or cut off the probation list, they are faced with an array of decisions. Arguably, then, they would be better equipped to make sensible decisions if they had some practical experience. In addition, because many offenders may have made poor decisions prior to their apprehension, the correctional experience—although it might accomplish nothing else—might provide qualitative decision-making experiences—perhaps this is one of the benefits of the "contracting" experiments.

Beyond this, the provision of certain prisoner protections at each key decision point in the correctional process undoubtedly will impart some greater sense of justice and fairness than the anarchy that generally prevails. For offenders whose lives (or at least whose perceptions of their lives) have not been characterized by "fairness," experiencing some minimal fairness while they are subject to restraint might impress them.

Prisoners' rights have been and will be vigorously resisted by prison management—security and stability are compromised when a prisoner exercises a previously unavailable right. Yet disciplinary decisions, and even more profoundly, parole decisions, have a powerful impact on an offender's life and well-being. As such it is argued that some reasonable set of due process protections should be afforded. This isn't the place to discuss what they should be or how they should be implemented. The point here is that such protections might alter the correctional experience for some offenders in such a way that their behavior after release might be altered. This is one more thing that we don't know, but it is certainly worth exploring.

Notes

1. Marvin E. Frankel, *Criminal Sentences* (New York: Hill & Wang, 1973), p. 5.

2. Erik Olin Wright, *The Politics of Punishment* (New York: Harper & Row, 1973), p. 33.

3. Marvin Wolfgang and Bernard Cohen, *Race and Crime* (New York: Institute of Human Relations Press, 1970).

4. See *Report of the National Advisory Commission on Civil Disorders* (New York: Bantam, 1968); and National Commission on the Causes and Prevention of Violence, *Staff Report*, vol. 12 (Washington, D.C.: Government Printing Office, 1968).

5. See Gunnar Marnell, "Comparative Correctional Systems: U.S. and Sweden," *Criminal Law Bulletin* 8 (1972):748-760; and Norval Morris, "Lessons from the Adult Correctional System of Sweden," *Federal Probation* 30 (December 1966):3-13.

6. Morris, "Lessons from the Adult Correctional System," p. 4. Reprinted with permission.

7. *Los Angeles Times*, May 16, 1975.

8. Jessica Mitford, *Kind and Usual Punishment* (New York: Knopf, 1973), p. 86.

9. See, for example, James O. Robison, *Rehabilitating Parole* (Berkeley, Calif.: Criminological Research Associates, 1974).

10. See William J. Genego, Peter D. Goldberger, and Vicki C. Jackson, "Parole Release Decision-Making and the Sentencing Process," *Yale Law Journal* 84 (March 1975):810-902.

11. Citizens' Inquiry Board on New York Parole and Criminal Justice, Inc., *Prison Without Walls: Report on New York Parole*, (New York: Praeger Publishers, Inc., 1975), pp. xx, 176.

12. *New York Times Magazine*, May 28, 1972, pp. 14ff.

13. Lloyd Ohlin and Frank Remington, "Sentencing Structure: Its Effect Upon Systems for the Administration of Criminal Justice," *Law and Contemporary Problems* 23 (Summer 1958):495-507.

14. See National Advisory Commission on Criminal Justice Standards and Goals, *Task Force Report: Corrections* (Washington, D.C.: Government Printing Office, 1975).

15. *Los Angeles Times*, February 8, 1975, Part I, p. 19.

16. See Citizens' Inquiry Board, *Prison Without Walls*.

17. Daniel Glaser, "Criminology and Public Policy," *American Sociologist* (June 1971):30-37.

18. Isaac Ehrlich, "The Deterrent Impact of Capital Punishment: A Question of Life and Death," *American Economic Review* 65 (June 1975):397-417, especially p. 398. For some of the critical reactions, see "Study Saying Executions Defer Murder Stirs Furor," *Los Angeles Times*, May 5, 1975, Part I, p. 1.

19. Robert Martinson, "What Works?—Questions and Answers About Prison Reform," *The Public Interest* 35 (Spring 1974):41.

20. California Youth Authority, "The Status of Current Research in the CYA and Delinquency Control Project—L.A. Study: Project Report" (Sacramento, May 1968).

21. See James Q. Wilson, "If Every Criminal Knew He Would Be Punished if Caught," *New York Times Magazine*, January 29, 1973, p. 9ff.

22. Franklin Zimring, "Measuring the Impact of Pretrial Diversion from the Criminal Justice System," *University of Chicago Law Review* 41 (1974):241.

23. Nora Klapmuts, "Diversion from the Criminal Justice System," *Crime and Delinquency Literature* (March 1975):108-131.

24. Elizabeth W. Vorenberg and James Vorenberg, "Early Diversion from the Criminal Justice System: Practice in Search of a Theory," in Lloyd Ohlin, ed., *Prisoners in America* (Englewood Cliffs, N.J.: Prentice-Hall, 1973), p. 161.

25. Ibid., pp. 177 ff.

26. Robert Martinson, "What Works?—Questions and Answers About Prison Reform," *The Public Interest* 35 (Spring 1974). See also Douglas S. Lipton, Robert Martinson, and Judith Wilks, *The Effectiveness of Correctional Treatment: A Survey of Treatment Evaluation Studies* (New York: Praeger, 1975).

27. Ibid., p. 69. Reprinted with permission.

28. Ibid.

29. Frank Tannenbaum, quoted in William Nagel, *The New Red Barn* (New York: Walker, 1973), p. 148.

30. Nagel, *The Red Barn*, p. 147. Reprinted with permission.

31. Edward Eldefonso, *Issues in Corrections* (Beverly Hills, Calif.: Glencoe Press, 1974).

32. See note k, p. 97.

33. See, for example, Klapmuts, "Diversion from the Criminal Justice System."

34. "Pretrial Intervention: A Cost-Benefit Analysis," in *Cost-Benefit Analysis: Three Applications to Corrections* (Washington, D.C.: Correctional Economic Center, American Bar Association, May 1974), pp. 19-21.

35. Ibid., pp. 22-23.

36. See Raymond T. Nimmer, *Diversion: The Search for Alternative Forms of Prosecution* (Chicago: American Bar Foundation, 1974).

37. See, for example, Vorenberg and Vorenberg, "Early Diversion."

38. See "The Crime Wave," *Time*, June 30, 1975, p. 22.

39. See Morris, "Lessons from the Adult Correctional System."

40. See, for example, Edward W. Bohlander, "Shock Probation: The Use and Effectiveness of an Early Release Program as a Sentencing Alternative" (Ann Arbor, Mich.: University Microfilms, 1973).

41. Norval Morris, *The Future of Imprisonment* (Chicago: University of Chicago Press, 1974), p. 18.

42. Maryland Annual Code, Art. 31B, Section 5, 1975. Quoted in Andrew Von Hirsch, "Prediction of Criminal Conduct and Preventive Confinement of Convicted Persons," *Buffalo Law Review* 21 (1972):717.

43. Norval Morris, *The Future of Imprisonment* (Chicago: University of Chicago Press, 1974), p. 34. Reprinted by permission of The University of Chicago Press.

44. National Advisory Commission on Criminal Justice Standards and Goals, *Task Force Report: Corrections* (Washington, D.C.: Government Printing Office, 1973), p. 107. Reprinted with permission.

45. Morris, *Future of Imprisonment*, pp. 79-80. Reprinted by permission of the University of Chicago Press. Copyright by the University of Chicago Press.

46. For a preliminary discussion of the issue "minus the false positives," see Von Hirsch, "Prediction of Criminal Conduct," pp. 744ff.

47. From a letter to Philip Zimbardo, in "Prisons, Prison Reform, and Prisoners' Rights: California," Hearings before Subcommittee No. 3 of the Committee on the Judiciary, House of Representatives, 92nd Congress, 1st Sess., on Corrections, Part II, October 25, 1971 (Washington, D.C.: Government Printing Office, 1971), p. 110.

48. Albert F. Nussbaum, "The Rehabilitation Myth," *The American Scholar* 40 (Autumn 1971):674-675. Copyright © 1971 by United Chapters of Phi Beta Kappa. By permission of publishers.

49. Citizens' Inquiry Board, *Prison Without Walls*, p. 29.

50. For an explanation of the proposal, see Don M. Gottfredson, Peter B. Hoffman, Maurice H. Sigler and Leslie T. Wilkins, "Making Parole Policy Explicit," *Crime and Delinquency* 21 (January 1975):34-44.

51. See American Correctional Association, "The Mutual Agreement Program: A Planned Change in Correctional Service Delivery" (College Park, Md., 1973).

52. See, for example, "Bargaining in Correctional Institutions: Restructuring the Relation between the Inmate and the Prison Authority," *Yale Law Journal* 81 (1972):726.

53. See, for example, "Restitutive Justice: A General Survey and Analysis," a report submitted to the National Institute of Law Enforcement and Criminal Justice by Battelle, Inc., Herbert Edelhertz, Project Director. See also "The Minnesota Restitution Center," *Corrections Magazine* 1, no. 3 (July/August 1975):13.

54. See, for example, Herbert Edelhertz and Gilbert Geis, *Public Compensation to Victims of Crime* (New York: Praeger, 1974).

55. "The Crime Wave," *Time*, quoting Harold MacEwen, June 30, 1975, p. 10. Reprinted by permission from *TIME*, The Weekly Newsmagazine; copyright Time, Inc.

6 Where to from Here?

There have been numerous arguments that we have reached the "end of ideology", that we no longer have a prevailing ideological perspective that guides our evolution. This seems to be the case in corrections. The idea that nothing works is emerging as a powerful belief, but it lacks theoretical stature. Instead, it is more of a recognition that nothing has yet been found that works. The search for a unifying theory continues, and the search for something that works continues as well. But no one theory has excited corrections with a new mission.

The reform proposals of today, when taken together, are broadly eclectic. Because of patent inhumanities, some of the severities of prison life have been moderated. Because of the failures of treatment, rehabilitation has been discredited. Because of a belief that the community is a better place to correct than the country, correctional programs are slowly being shifted to the community. Because of the conviction that prisons are too large, in some jurisdictions inmate populations are being slowly reduced. And because there is a small body of empirical evidence, deterrence can be merchandised once again.

None of these developments can be patched together to make a whole, much less a whole greater than the sum of the parts. They are not derived from some corpus of theory about how to treat the crime problem. Each has its own sponsorship, its own constituency. There is no theoretical glue to hold them together.

One of the most obvious dilemmas of reform is that between reforming the system and developing a new model for the system. In part this is a recapitulation of the debate between "working within the system" versus "radical change." But beyond that, there is the question of whether to attempt a change in correctional ideology or to stick more closely to pragmatic goals.

The chief appeal of the "reforms" method is that it promises direct action toward what seems most obviously needed. It doesn't require "true believers" in any one theory, but rather it appeals to anyone who shares a distaste for specific abuses. In addition, success in one area does not depend on success in another; for example, plea-bargaining and its inequities still might remain, even though parole was replaced by a system with shorter fixed terms.

The "model-builders," on the other hand, offer us an intellectual basket in which to carry the various reform proposals. By giving the system a new structure (whichever one it might be), many of the current contradictions and inconsistencies might naturally disappear—certain changes would be forced by the new broom's clean sweep. Nevertheless, we are leery of the ideological bandwagon, however attractive it might appear. Rehabilitation promised similar sweeping changes in the 1870s, and today we have little to show for it.

Theory has offered too much and too little. In its grandiose and philosophical form, it says so much that discrete events get lost and the real world dissolves. It's as if there were an irreducible set of building blocks for theoreticians to play with. Each assembles them somewhat differently and occasionally, to throw critics off, calls them by different names. This process can work for a long time if the number of blocks is relatively limitless. But in criminology there don't seem to be that many blocks. The fundamental ones are free will, determinism, a focus on the individual or society, consensual versus conflictive views of society—and separate blocks for social defense, deterrence, retribution, rehabilitation, etc. Some blocks don't fit together, some only partially fit, and still others fit reasonably well.

Most theoreticians refuse to play with all the blocks—they choose some and then stick with them even though the picture they convey might be skewed. All theoreticians find something wrong with someone else's building. And yet although there have been a few attempts to construct a building that everyone would like, no one has done so. We haven't constructed a theory that explains what we're trying to do. It can probably be done, though, unless we're missing some blocks.

So where are we today? We have seen the slow resuscitation of classical thinking about crime and corrections. It is characterized by a new interest in punishment for its own sake, and in just deserts or retribution. This interest stems from our disenchantment with the rehabilitative ideal and our frustrations with social theory. Our disenchantment with rehabilitation arises from its failure to deliver on its promises. And we are frustrated with social theory, first because it is so elegantly abstract, and second, because its diagnoses, however accurate, leave us few realistic prescriptions for action. Thus in our flight from treating either the individual or society, we yearn for simple remedies that will in turn yield simple aims for corrections. But how far are we prepared to go? Are we going to argue for punishment to fit the crime and for the principle of just deserts as a ceiling on all punishment, and then leave it up to judges to implement our wishes without constraining their choices? And as long as the "technology" of treatment is around, it will be difficult not to use it—this implies that mitigation will always operate. Moreover, we seem to have an insatiable taste for prediction. It too will limit our desires for uniformity.

Then, also, as long as we recognize the need to restrain some—the irreducible residue—principles of social defense will compel us to keep the prison for at least this number, whatever it may be. And as long as we have the prison, we also may be tempted to use it. Ultimately, reductions in the prison population and in sentence lengths may in fact require bulldozing the prison.[a]

[a]This was Jerry Miller's experience in Massachusetts. See Andrew Rutherford, "The Dissolution of the Training Schools in Massachusetts" (Columbus, Ohio: Academy for Contemporary Problems, 1974); and Lloyd Ohlin, Robert B. Coates and Allen D. Miller, "Radical Correctional Reform: A Case Study of the Massachusetts Youth Correctional System," *Harvard Education Review*, 44, no. 1, 1974.

And what about judicial discretion? The continual exercise of broad discretion by judges will nullify any attempt to introduce classical principles into punishment even if the judiciary can be philosophically convinced that punishment should fit the crime.

Finally, there is the question of the community. Despite years of chatter about the community as a base for corrections, almost nothing has happened. The movement is alive and well, and if the literature is to be believed, the streets must already be teeming with offenders. But that is simply not the case. At best, there is a slow trickle from the country to the city. And the reason is that we don't know what we're talking about when we talk about the community—and further, because the advocates of the community can prove neither that it will work nor that it will be more humane, nor that it will represent less instead of more social control.

So again, where are we? As usual, there is a gap between theory and practice. The gap may be closing slowly, but the result is unlikely to be a convergence. Instead we almost necessarily are moving into an area of compromise and consolidation. Because we have no new theory to galvanize us, we choose instead to chop off the extremes that have characterized past practices based on outmoded theory. Hence we curb the indetermediate sentence; we seek to reduce the length of sentences, recognizing our relative barbarism vis-à-vis other cultures; we seek to humanize the prison experience further; and we seek to limit the use of the prison by speculating on the use of the city. We appear to be choosing to go with what seems best, whatever its theoretical origin and whatever its lineage.

Reform and Reform Movements

Most of the major reforms have been identified. They include

1. more uniformity in sentencing
2. reduction or elimination of coercive treatment
3. wider use of the community for correctional programs
4. less reliance on the prison (in a few instances, elimination of the prison)
5. limiting the prison to the custody of only those who are too violent to release
6. greater use of probation
7. reorganization and perhaps less reliance on parole
8. reductions in the length of sentences
9. elimination or substantial modification of the indeterminate sentence
10. richer voluntary correctional program opportunities
11. further expansion of prisoners' rights and privileges
12. more "humanization" of correctional practices
13. more attention to crimes committed by population cohorts that have been historically "underrepresented" in the offender pool

14. restrictions on plea-bargaining
15. decriminalization
16. wider use of diversion programs.

The Recommendations of the Major Commissions

Calls for reform are by no means new. Since the Wickersham Commission in 1931, a long list of prestigious commissions have recommended substantial changes in the criminal justice system. Any discussion of these recommendations would be very lengthy. Table 6-1 condenses the major recommendations of each of six commissions in tabular form.[b]

The tabulation leaves a lot of detail and nuance out, but it makes a few observations possible. First, there is striking unanimity; in fact, most of the differences in the recommendations appear to be attributable to the differences in the time of the report issuance rather than to any imputed ideological difference. For example, the Wickersham Commission, which published its findings in 1931, included a recommendation that "an indeterminate sentence is necessary for the development of a proper institutional program and an essential to the establishment of an adequate system of parole.[1] But more recently, the indeterminate sentence has been flatly opposed, most notably by the American Friends Service Committee in *Struggle for Justice*.[2] Even the very recent Standards and Goals Commission would sharply limit the indeterminate sentence by imposing a five-year ceiling on sentencing, except in the case of homicide.[3]

This "drift" of recommendations as a function of time is the most obvious in four instances: plea-bargaining, construction of new correctional facilities, prisoners' rights and privileges, and the use of the indeterminate sentence. The three most recent commissions—the Council on Economic Development, the Standards and Goals Commission, and the "Friends"—oppose the use of plea-bargaining. Both the Friends and the Standards and Goals Commission oppose further construction of penal facilities, and all the commissions have championed expanded prisoners' rights and privileges, although with some variations. And with the exception of the Standards and Goals Commission, all three oppose the use of the indeterminate sentence, although as noted, the Standards and Goals Commission would undercut its use substantially.

Beyond the consensus on specific recommendations, the rhetoric is also comparable: shock couched in civility. For example, almost all agree that the existing correctional system has failed miserably; most agree that it punishes too severely and inequitably; most, that it doesn't (or can't) correct; and most, that

[b]The commissions were not interested in exactly the same set of issues; some had yet to arise at the time of the Wickersham Commission, whereas others were resolved by the seventies. In addition, different areas were chosen for attention: the Von Hirsch report deals specifically with sentencing, whereas the Council on Economic Development addressed the criminal justice system as a whole.

Table 6-1
Summary of the Six Major Commissions' Recommendations

Recommendations	Wickersham Commission (1931)	Crime in a Free Society (1967)	American Friends Service Committee (1971)	Council on Economic Development (1972)	Standards and Goals Commission (1973)	Committee for the Study of Incarceration (1975)
The Criminal Justice "Net"						
Decriminalization of "victimless" crime		+	+	+	+	+
Increased use of pretrial diversion		+		+		
Use of plea-bargaining		+	0	0	0	
Sentencing						
Reduction of sentence lengths		+		+	+	+
Sparing use of incarceration	+	+	+	+	+	+
Greater uniformity of sentences	0	+	+	+	+	+
Use of indeterminate sentence	+		0	+	0	0
The Prison						
Construction of new, improved institutions	+	+	+	0	0	0
Better classification and diagnosis of offenders	+	+		+		
Improvement of disciplinary procedures	+	+		+	+	
Increased resources for prison rehabilitation	+	+	+	+		0
Repeal of laws prohibiting sale of prison-made goods	0	+		+	+	

+ = Favors;
0 = Opposes

it must "shift" to the community somehow. There are ideological differences and different emphases between the Friends' *Struggle for Justice*, for example, and the report of the Commission on Standards and Goals. But their overlap on the problems of the current system is substantial, and their use of ringing rhetoric is striking. These excerpts are illustrative:

It is clear that a dramatic realignment of correctional methods is called for. It is essential to abate the use of institutions. Meanwhile much can be done to eliminate the worst effects of the institution—its crippling idleness, anonymous brutality, and destructive impact . . . .[4]

The failure of major institutions to reduce crime is incontestable. Recidivism rates are notoriously high. Institutions do succeed in punishing, but they do not deter.[5]

Despite the force of many of the proposals, and despite their unanimity, there is still something missing. There is an absence of rationale, of cement or framework. Most of the recommendations are "reactions" to past abuses, not prescriptions for future successes. The indeterminate sentence is opposed because it didn't work. But the fixed sentence is not actively promoted in its place because there is no firm belief in its power. No, only more uniformity is proposed, leaving the "more" to subsequent definition. The same is the case with sentencing. Shorter sentences are proposed because the evidence suggests that they will work as well as longer ones. But work as well at what? Presumably, what is meant is that the recidivism rate isn't affected by the length of a prisoner's term (or apparently, by anything else). If there are other reasons for shorter sentences, such as humanism or reintegration, they are rarely articulated.

So once again, the gap between theory and practice yawns. None of the commissions has supplied a philosophical framework within which to set its ideas; instead each has strewn the ground with a series of recommendations with the hope that some of them might be picked up.

Models of Correctional Reform

Given the drift, we are exploring some new and some refurbished models for corrections of the future. Obviously there are a number of ways to conceptualize corrections. For example, Vincent O'Leary generated a set of four models of correctional practice; his tabular representation of the models is reprinted as Table 6-2. O'Leary's conclusion was that only reintegration is a suitable purpose for corrections because "only reintegration is, by nature, open."[6] Eric H. Steele

Table 6-2
Models of Correctional Policies

		Emphasis on the Community	
		Low	High
Emphasis on the Offender — High		Rehabilitation (Identification Focus)	Reintegration (Internalization Focus)
Emphasis on the Offender — Low		Restraint (Organizational Focus)	Reform (Compliance Focus)

Reform Model:　　　　　high emphasis on the community; low emphasis on the offender.
Rehabilitation Model:　low emphasis on the community; high emphasis on the offender.
Restraint Model:　　　　low emphasis on the community; low emphasis on the offender.
Reintegration Model:　high emphasis on the community; high emphasis on the offender.

Source: Vincent O'Leary, "Correctional Policy: A Classification of Goals Designed for Change," *Crime and Delinquency* 17 (October 1971):384. Reprinted with permission of the National Council on Crime and Delinquency.

and James Jacobs have constructed a typology on the basis of the type of prison organization employed. The "hierarchical" system is reform/control-oriented; the "differentiated" system focuses on specialized treatment facilities; and the "autonomous" system is along the lines of the "justice model" theories.[7]

These models are valuable as ways of intellectually organizing the parts of the system. But the purpose of the model-building that follows is not to present the most rigorous conceptualization possible, but to frame the models in terms of what is really happening. In the real world of correctional policy-makers and politics, there are some models emerging that have attracted allegiance. The models listed here, then, are those that have already stimulated a relatively high level of political debate. They are not my creations; they already exist in the literature. None has yet captured enough imagination to be compelling; none is that comprehensive. All have been described in some detail in previous sections. They will be briefly described below, and then we will ask whether they will work.

The Functionalist Model. This is not so much a model of correctional practice; as it is an explanation of the phenomenon of crime. The explanation has many adherents, and it has significant implications for correctional practice, on the assumption that it is valid. To the extent to which it is accurate, it suggests that law enforcement can affect only marginally crime rates and that the correctional system will continue to receive a relatively unvarying flow of offenders.

The Rehabilitative Model. This model has attracted the most adherents in recent decades, but has come under intense fire in the last few years. Its repudiation has stemmed from a lack of evidence of treatment—none of the technology utilized in the model works.

The Retribution Model. In the wake of the rehabilitative model's retreat, the retribution model has reemerged. It enjoys a swelling amount of support even though it has not yet been fully formulated.

The Deterrence Model. A renewed interest in the deterrent effect of punishment is leading to the derivation of a model of correctional practice that would be based on the demonstrable deterrent effect of various correctional devices.

The Reintegration Model. The proponents of rehabilitation don't give up easily. But recognizing the defects in and the ineffectiveness of rehabilitation, they have formulated a new model that retains a treatment orientation but stresses the importance of abandoning the prison and basing most correctional programs in the community.

The Justice Model.[c] Related to the functionalist perspective, this model also removes rehabilitative goals and is premised on the introduction of due process protections to the inmate and the promotion of specified inmate rights.

How Do the Models Fit Together?

Elements of all the models are competing for loyalty. But they don't blend together that well. The overlap in premises and objectives is fairly slim.

Rehabilitation and Reintegration. The rehabilitative and reintegrative models are largely compatible, but they differ on where corrections should occur. Proponents of reintegration recognize the futility of attempting to treat anyone in the artificial and coercive conditions of the prison, and hence they stress the reintegration of the offender into the community. But what community and what techniques would be used to do so?

Many offenders may have no community to return to—particularly if "community" defined less in geographic terms and more in terms of intimate, nurturant contacts. Our thinking about communities is not only shallow, but perhaps provincial as well. We tend to think of community as either a family or a nation with very little in between. But many, offenders included, have no family, if they do, it may not be nurturant. And many, offenders again included, have little fidelity to large institutions like the church, school, government, and even employers. This leaves a void, unless there are intermediate communities to which offenders might relate. These might be community centers, neighborhood clubs, Synanon-like centers, and more diffuse networks of individuals and groups that, although they are hard to define, may yield identity to many who seek it. If this is so, reintegration must not be falsely premised on the existence and effectiveness of communities that do not or may not exist. For at least some offenders, perhaps the majority, community must be either created or at least stimulated. The community corrections center discussed on pp. 000-000 might be a start, as might "voucher" programs that use existing volunteer groups.

The location question has never been resolved either. Some offenders may have no roots; others who do have roots may find their return to those roots more compromising than a fresh start; and still others may prefer to remain rootless. If this is so, then the community corrections movement should retain

---

[c]A seventh model—incapacitation—could be added. All the talk about "locking them up," most recently manifested in President Ford's message to congress on criminal justice and law enforcement, arises from this notion. Yet incapacitation is a necessary function of any model of correctional practice to the extent to which any restraints are placed on the offender. Moreover, few who argue for incapacitation as a "purpose" for corrections also argue that once offenders are restrained that nothing further should be done, or that their incapacitation doesn't serve other ends, such as deterrence, retribution, and so forth. Hence I will refer to incapacitation here as a parameter of other models of practice rather than as an encompassing rationale for that practice.

some flexibility and not automatically deposit offenders on the same street where they were apprehended. In some cases relocation programs, with the offender's consent, might be considered, especially when a community that isn't the offender's own may possess more appropriate resources.

As to techniques, it is hard to identify treatment technologies that will differ from those that have already been examined and found wanting. Advocates of reintegration still must face the argument that treatment is a very limited tool, even though they propose to abandon the prison as a laboratory. Further, the means must still be found to strip treatment of coerciveness, even within the community, if it is assumed that the inherent coerciveness of the prison emasculated treatment in that setting. Arguably, then, if treatment results in the community are linked with release from the program, the absence of bars, locks, and guards may make no difference.

Neither the reintegration nor the rehabilitation model has found a solution for either the dangerous or habitual offender. In rehabilitative thinking—as long as it remains prison-based—the problem isn't acute because most such dangerous offenders are presumably under detention and may simply be offenders who are most resistant to therapeutic intervention. But in the reintegration model, with its stress on community-based corrections, the question must be faced because it must be determined which offenders to release to the community and which not to. This too is an example of the relationship of incapacitation to the other models of corrections. If a formula is devised for the incarceration of dangerous/habitual offenders, their incapacitation meets the requirement of that model.

The indeterminate sentence has long been a constant companion of rehabilitation, because without it, therapists lacked the tool to enforce their treatment regimen.[d] But as the rehabilitation model wanes, the indeterminate sentence—or more accurately, indeterminacy—is being reduced. A more fixed sentence doesn't preclude rehabilitation, but it undercuts the therapist's authority to decide when the offender has been cured, and it substantially weakens the inmate's resolve to cooperate with authority because his or her release is no longer tied to program participation so intimately.

The same is true for reintegration. If the period of community-based treatment is fixed, a substantial amount of "leverage" over the offender is lost. But in addition, reintegration in the community, as opposed to rehabilitation in the prison, poses security problems that have yet to be recognized fully. Reintegration is premised on easing the offender back into a supportive community, presumably because the offender will be given the opportunity to establish supportive relationships. But this opportunity could be compromised easily by unduly rigid security measures. And, as noted earlier, lax security is unlikely if citizen objections are pitched—and they are likely to be pitched. Yet

---

[d]Invariably to many, the indeterminate sentence also turned out to be an "incapacitative" tool because the length of sentence generally increased in proportion to the indeterminacy of the sentence. See Jessica Mitford, *Kind and Usual Punishment* (New York: Knopf, 1973).

if offenders in the community aren't circumscribed to a noticeable degree, the deterrent impact of community-based corrections undoubtedly will be less than imprisonment. This is a clear tradeoff, and it should be acknowledged as such.

One distinct advantage of the reintegration formula is that it affords the opportunity to shift some responsibility for "outcome" to the offender. In rehabilitation—even if it were an objective, which it rarely is—the inherent coerciveness of the prison stripped responsibility of any meaning. But in the community it is possible. Reintegration need not be inflexibly wed to the medical model, which deprives the patient/offender of any responsibility for well-being. Reintegration could free itself from the dead hand of that model and experiment with shifting responsibility to the offender. It might link itself with the burgeoning practice of inmate contracting.

One of the often unarticulated premises of both rehabilitation and reintegration, particularly if reintegration is rich in program possibilities, is that they are "compensatory" systems. They are premised in part on remedying defects in offender makeup that are hereditary or environmental or both. There is thus an implicit recognition that an offender's conduct is not wholly the product of individual choice—that circumstances and conditions may influence individual choice, or in some cases compel certain behavior. It may be true that rehabilitation cannot be made to work for offenders as a whole, but to abandon it for that reason alone may strip successor programs of some symbolic content—not just for the offender, who might perceive a certain "meanness" in society's refusal to offer any help, but also for society itself, which may experience a certain "meanness" in failing to offer it.

Retribution and Deterrence. Because rehabilitation has been gutted, its surrogate—the reintegration model—is now competing with the retribution, deterrence, and incapacitation models for the allegiance of correctional decision-makers. Conceding the failures and frustrations of rehabilitation, many now advocate a return to a calculation of "just deserts," and concomitantly, an abandonment of attempts to reform the wayward. The correlates of this theory at the level of practice are the fixed term or sentence, retention of the prison, and fewer programmatic frills, especially those designed to "change" the offender. The shift is most sharply stated by James Q. Wilson:

Now suppose we abandon entirely the rehabilitation theory of sentencing and corrections—not the *effort* to rehabilitate, just the theory that the governing purpose of the enterprise is to rehabilitate. We could continue experiments with new correctional and therapeutic procedures, expanding them when the evidence warrants. If existing correctional programs do not differ in their rehabilitative potential, we could support those that are least costly and most humane (while still providing reasonable security) and phase out those that are most costly and inhumane. But we would not do any of these things on the mistaken notion that we were thereby reducing recidivism.

Instead, we would view the correctional system as having a very different function—namely, to isolate and to punish.[8,e]

The retribution model is appealing in its simplicity. But it requires a rationale that transcends its character as a "reaction" to the rehabilitation model's failure. The Committee for the Study of Incarceration, in the most comprehensive conceptualization to date,[9] struggled with this problem and finally settled on a sort of "natural justice" rationale: The offender must be punished because to fail to do so would erode the moral sense of the community.[f] This formulation, however valid philosophically, may fail to satisfy very many people. On the other hand, few people probably care one way or the other—they are interested in retribution only as a solution to a short-term problem. But this leaves the model at the level of expediency. Ultimately, if retribution is to be viable as a purpose of punishment, a rationale will have to be developed which is consistent with the thinking of those who empower and guide the correctional system. Perhaps a consensus will emerge, but it hasn't yet. Taking aim at such a consensus has been a problem because of the power of the rehabilitative theory, and because "punishment for punishment's sake," which is the way retribution is often interpreted, is unpalatable to many.

Beyond the question of rationale, the retributive formula poses a host of practical problems. In theory, once retribution is accepted as the raison d'être, the modalities of correction are open to choice as long as they don't violate the fundamental notions of just deserts. In other words, at the purely theoretical level, the retribution model doesn't compel the use of the prison or the community. Yet these questions have not been worked out, partially because most proposals advocating a return to retribution as a purpose for punishment—including the work of the Committee for the Study of Incarceration—have focused on the reform of sentencing, not the reconceptualization of correctional practice. But this strategy may backfire—the rehabilitative model may sneak in through the back door even with the diminution in judicial discretion in sentencing. For example, most fixed-term proposals incorporate "good-time" provisions. But what will be defined as good time? If program participation, whether voluntary or not, is tied to good-time credits, the retributive formula will have been watered down.[g] More sharply, is it likely that state legislatures will purge the judiciary of

[e]Wilson's observation also fits "incapacitation" objectives in its emphasis on the protection of society.

[f]One problem with the committee's formulation is that it strays somewhat from the historical conception of the retributive idea. Conventionally, retribution meets society's needs for fairness and symmetry—if X does Y, and Y is prohibited, presumably society has been harmed (the reasons why Y is prohibited) and hence society has a right to punish X. But in the committee's work, the rationale has become more complex. Somehow the idea is that the individual must be punished for his or her own sake, as if to fail to do so fails the individual as much or more than society. There's nothing wrong with this, it's just that the committee seems to have relied more heavily on Kant than on anyone else.

[g]The Committee for the Study of Incarceration recognized this and argued for limits to good-time provisions, or else we would see a return to "the Chinese water torture of uncertainty." See the committee's report, *The Justice of Punishment*.

any and all discretion in sentencing? It may be plausible to argue that indeterminacy can be diminished; but will it be eliminated?

What would be the effect of a return to retribution on the length of sentences imposed and actually served? Sentences in the United States, as noted earlier, are longer than in most Western European countries. But the rehabilitation model, with all its flexibility, had the advantage (paired with many disadvantages) of allowing the judiciary to impose seemingly long sentences to placate public opinion, while at the same time tolerating substantial modulation of those sentences by parole boards.[10] With the return to statutorily fixed terms, however, great pressure will be exerted on state legislatures to fix terms that will be at least as long as the maxima under today's indeterminate statutes, *but* without provision for moderation, except in the case of good time. Hence the dilemma: If good-time provisions are generous, the indeterminate sentence may in fact return in different garb, and with it rehabilitative practices; but if good-time provisions are lean, the average duration of sentences may increase. Of course, this is not necessarily inconsistent with retributive thinking, although it may discomfort some of its proponents. Ultimately, if retribution is more than elitist engineering, the public, gluttonous or not, is supposed to decide on its "pound of flesh." In the past, if we took a pound, most of the time twelve ounces was refunded through the play of indeterminacy and rehabilitative corrections. Now the public may choose to take the pound without any refund.

There is nothing irresolvably inconsistent between retributive concepts and reintegration programs. If society has chosen its price, it doesn't follow that the price must be paid in the prison. It may, but conceptually, community-based correctional programs can be used to execute retributive objectives. However, for reintegration to work, a high degree of flexibility is required. But flexibility may not be possible under the retribution rubric, especially if deterrent purposes are to be met as well—and deterrence is conceptually close to the retribution model.

As long as only some serve their terms in prison, the "dangerousness" question is posed. But in the context of retribution, the issue takes on a shine. The principle of just deserts presupposes that a formula can be derived to match the punishment with the damage inflicted on society. But where in this formula is there room for the extraordinary penalty—the long-term incarceration of the dangerous offender? Can society exact a higher price just because an offender has been classified (with considerable caprice) as dangerous, and if so, how is the penalty calculated? If the dangerous offender is simply one who because of past behavior is more dangerous as a matter of degree, an "extraordinary" penalty is hard to fit with the retributive rationale. In other words, it may be hard to justify a "premium" on the penalty for offender X just because she has committed five offenses when offender Y, who has committed only four, doesn't get the same treatment. But if the dangerous offender is somehow different in character, or if his or her repeated offenses are evidence of greater culpability, a special penalty might be justified.[11]

Whether the retribution formula includes extraordinary penalties or not, the general deterrent impact of retributive sentencing—if it isn't diluted by mitigation and if the prison retains a prominent role—should be greater than in the current system. Whether this would also be true with specific deterrence is much harder to say, unless terms served turn out to be statistically longer and are perceived as such by the specific offender.

The role of the prison under retributive thinking would probably remain large. And it isn't inconceivable that some sort of modest shift to the community might occur. However, given the relative "softness" of community-based corrections, retributive objectives would be better served if the prison system were retained.[12] This doesn't necessarily mean that prisons might not be renovated, newly constructed, or relocated, but it does mean that fixed terms are more easily implemented in the prison because security can be reasonably assured and deterrence is likely to be more effective.

Retribution is highly compatible with deterrence, but is not the same. There is a different model of practice emerging under the deterrence rubric. To the retributionist, the offender is not the important variable—there is no intent to "cure" those who become enmeshed in the system. Rather, as with deterrence, the offender serves as the currency in the bargain between the government and the people. In retribution, the bargain is that the government will allow the public to set the price the offender should pay, and then will fulfill its end of the deal by punishing the offender to the extent the people want. In the deterrence model, the nature and extent of punishment is again part of the bargain, but in this case the offender will be punished to the extent that it will deter the general public from the commission of a like offense and will, as well, deter the offender from further criminal conduct, irrespective of society's formulation of just deserts. In each case the offender has a symbolic value—a value that transcends any specific program designed to help him or her.

But there are some differences. In the calculation of the deterrent formulas, the test is what will work—what amount of punishment, of almost whatever severity, will demonstrably deter. The "price" in terms of the public attitudes that retribution seeks to capture is irrelevant. The same is true for the retributionist—once the level of punishment has been set, if it serves deterrent objectives, it might be nice, but not necessary. The test in the deterrence model is empirical—the test in retribution is social, although it might be derived by empirical means.

In terms of practice this means that there is no theoretical limit to the length of sentence in the deterrence model, whereas in retribution, the idea of just deserts supplies a ceiling, even though it may be hard to discern. And even if it turned out, by chance, that the length of sentence for X was the same under either model, the deterrence advocate still might opt for increased degrees of degradation to the offender, not necessarily out of malice, but because for deterrence to work the correctional experience must not only be hurtful, but also appear to be hurtful.[h] To the contrary, with retribution, once the "price" has been fixed, both social and individual needs have been met, presumably leaving correctional experience open to humanization.[i]

The resurgence of the deterrence model is partially the yield of recent econometric analysis in corrections. As noted on pp. 64-66, economists have been fascinated with punishment because it is one of the few laboratories where many of the variables can be manipulated. But whereas the model has heuristic value, it is difficult to operationalize. Society may not be willing to construct a correctional system that is sufficiently draconian to satisfy deterrent goals. And if it doesn't satisfy them, those who advocate deterrence will be left in the wings shouting for the rest of us to tighten the screws.

The Justice Model. The cold and calculating nature of both retribution and deterrence is inconsistent with reform movements that would extend offender responsibility, protect against discretionary abuses, and exercise expanded rights and privileges. While many of these reforms stem from limited concepts of correctional theory, they also can be subsumed under the justice model. This model is a reaction to the rehabilitative, retributionist, and deterrence formulations—to rehabilitation because it is so lawless, and to retribution and deterrence because they are so lifeless. It harkens to simple but powerful notions:

Justice can only be approached, never fully achieved. However, unless it is indeed the first virtue of the public institutions which administer it, none of the other virtues these institutions may possess will matter. . . . The removal of the assumptions which the belief in rehabilitation has engendered will make possible a system which will be more modest in aims, more rational in its means, and more just in its disposition.[13]

The model is conceptually related to the functionalist position because it does not assume that correction necessarily occurs, (or if it assumes that corrections can occur, it assumes it because correction is a felicitous by-product of just and humane treatment) but that nonetheless (or even because) the correctional experience could be made more humane. In stressing the offender's assumption of responsibility, in the context of due process protections, it is conceptually consistent with reintegration except that it promises no cures.

---

[h]As William C. Bailey puts it: "Fundamental to deterrence theory is the notion that potential offenders' *perceptions* of the probability of detection and the punishment that would result—no matter how mistaken—are the key mechanisms of deterrence" (emphasis in original). See "Crime and Deterrence: A Correlation Analysis," *Journal of Research in Crime and Delinquency* (July 1974):124-143, especially p. 140.

[i]This is why the retribution model can accommodate the justice model more easily—humanization of corrections is perfectly possible once the pricetag is on the crime.

The justice model can accommodate corrections in the community, as well as the retention of the prison for the demonstrably dangerous. But given its emphasis on due process, it is doubtful that any scheme for the detention of the dangerous would or could meet due process criteria. The model tends to break down at the program level. It's one thing to furnish safeguards against administrative abuse and to promote expanded offender rights, but yet another to introduce those rights and remedies into correctional programming. The justice model contemplates a prison with little or no remedial or rehabilitative programming, in part because such programs are coercive and demeaning, but also because inmate time is better spent litigating. Under the justice model, the prison is designed to inculcate inmate responsibility. The big questions, then, are: Is corrections merely custodial although it is drenched in due process, or will programs be offered—if so, what type? And if programs are offered, how is the trap that the retributionist also seeks to avoid avoided here—the trap of implementing programs that seek to cure?

There are other issues. Because the model doesn't compel (although it may favor) the community over the prison, questions about security, deterrence, and coercion don't loom so large. But what about the fixed term? Conceptually, the retributive fixed-term approach is more complementary to the justice model because it avoids the anarchy of rehabilitation. But with the fixed term, without any appreciable mitigating circumstances, what is there to fight about? Expanded offender rights such as assembly and free speech remain debatable, but if virtually nothing short of mayhem in the prison yard will alter the fixed term, the inmate is deprived of the opportunity to scrap and fight with the prison administration. And then what about expanded responsibility? One of the premises of the model is that fairness of treatment and widened responsibility will enhance the offender's experience once he or she is released. But with the fixed term there is very little for the offender to take responsibility for. At least with some "play" in his or her term, the offender can either contract for an early release or participate (or act as if participating) in correctional programs to enhance his or her prospects of an early release. Of course, the mind-bending aspect of rehabilitation is what the model seeks to escape, but in doing so a large measure of offender choice may be lost.

The justice model is less complete than the other models, save the functionalist model, which isn't a model at all, but really a caveat. In stressing offender rights and responsibilities it can be coupled with other objectives; but with some "fit" problems, it can be superimposed on a correctional system having other purposes.

The Models in Practice. A final means of comparing the models is to assess how one critical correctional issue would be handled under each model. The length of term is a good issue to take through.

To those who urge rehabilitation, the optimal length of term depends on the individual offender's needs—hence its offspring, the indeterminate sentence. Roughly the same is true with reintegration, except its proponents are less likely to favor indeterminacy. They, like the rehabilitators, desire some room within which to work—but because there is evidence that indeterminacy may wear down even the most malleable inmate's resolve to return to society, they are less enthusiastic.

The situation is very different with the deterrence model. Reform of the inmate is at best an incidental goal. Hence the optimal length of term is simply the term that can be shown to possess the greatest deterrent effect, however long it might be. Somewhat the same is the case with retribution. The length of term is not a curative choice, but instead a measure of what society chooses to exact as punishment, based on its desire to match the punishment with the gravity of the offense. Hence the term may be of almost any length, varying independently of any intent to reform or to deter. Its length is its length—as long as it is commensurate with society's sense of just deserts.

To those who believe that the purpose of corrections is to incapacitate, it follows that the longer the sentence, the better—unless, of course, some other simpler device, such as execution, exists. This objective is often softened in practice, but its philosophic consistency can't be doubted.

The justice model is distinguished from all the others in its emphasis on fairness and regularity. Theoretically, the length of sentence is not a parameter of the model. As long as due process protections are fully available to the offender, the sentence delivered by the court is immaterial—although it would be preferable if it weren't too harsh.

None of these perspectives finds its way into practice in pure form, although rehabilitation nearly succeeded in ousting all the others. Today the deterrence, retribution, and incapacitation approaches are suffusing the system, along with some aspects of the justice model. And, indeed, there is a danger in delineating models too cleanly. The impression is created, unless otherwise dispelled, that the models are independent or even contradictory. This is rarely the case in practice. They may be incompatible along some dimensions, as I have tried to show, but they can be blended into a kind of montage to reflect what appears to be an emerging consensus. The influence of each can be seen in the debate, and eventually in correctional practice itself. Yet these models of correctional practice, despite their inconsistencies, can be pasted together into a kind of "transitional" system. But it will be acutely unstable because some of its aims and some of its components will be at war with the others. The rehabilitation and reintegration models stress the central role of the community, therapeutic in part. The retribution model offers a rational model to reflect public perceptions of punishment, using the fixed term as a reflection of these perceptions. Those who argue for deterrence will insist on supplying empirically verifiable formulas to ensure that the punishment society chooses to dish out will have a suitable deterrent impact. And the justice model might provide the necessary constraints to administrative zeal under whatever banner is flown. (All the functionalists contribute is the reminder that it doesn't make any difference anyway.)

As unstable as the structure appears, it is the horse we're riding. But there is still time to ask if we want to go where it's heading.

The Recidivism of Inmate No. 1769. Sometime in the next few years Inmate no. 1769 will leave the prison. Someone will take his place, but possibly his cell may remain vacant for a while. But what is likely to happen to him if five years from now he is caught fencing some color TVs?

If 1769 is considered to be a dangerous offender, he may be put back in the prison. But because his haphazard offenses don't comprise a pattern as yet, and because no overt violence has been involved, he may be eligible for a "community" corrections program. He won't qualify for "special" diversion because he has accumulated too many offenses; but increasingly, diversion programs, once independent of the courts, are being absorbed into the correctional system to broaden the options available for disposition. As a result, 1769 may be eligible for a job-training program offered by a special job-training unit, once a part of a diversion program but now administered by the court. If he qualifies for training, he will be held in a minimum-security facility attached to the downtown courthouse complex.

If this program is filled, or if the judge doesn't think it is appropriate, for whatever reasons, 1769 will probably be required to check in with a community correctional facility attached to the downtown courthouse complex, and be assigned to the new medium-security facility a few miles outside town. Once there he may be asked to enter into a "contract" that will set the parameters of his program while he is imprisoned. In this case he then will be given special privileges to enroll in the first job-training program available, offered in the facility, with provision for on-the-job training on a furlough basis with a cooperating company in the city.

The length of 1769's sentence is two to four years, with provision for early release if he gets a job as a result of the job-training program. Provision is also made for good-time credits accumulating at the rate of one day for every one good-time day after the first six months. If he isn't released within two years, he will be up for parole. The parole board however, may, only formally consider his progress within the bounds of his "contract," along with any disciplinary actions, and it may not base its decision on the number or nature of any other programs in which 1769 has participated.

Although he has been released to the community, 1769 will be subject to frequent reporting requirements to be met by telephone contacts. If he fails to meet these requirements, he may be allowed further furlough privileges, but only if he agrees to electronic monitoring.

If 1769 errs anywhere along the line, beyond the modest tolerances imposed in his sentence, he will be sent back to the same cell he left five years before.

Notes

1. U.S. National Commission on Law Observance and Enforcement, *Reports* (Washington, D.C.: Government Printing Office, 1931), p. 172.

2. American Friends Service Committee, *Struggle for Justice* (New York: Hill & Wang, 1971).

3. National Advisory Commission on Criminal Justice Standards and Goals, *Task Force Report: Corrections* (Washington, D.C.: Government Printing Office, 1973), pp. 151-152.

4. AFSC, *Struggle for Justice.*

5. Standards and Goals Commission, *Task Force Report: Corrections*, p. 1.

6. Vincent O'Leary, "Correctional Policy: A Classification of Goals Designed for Change," *Crime and Delinquency* 17 (October 1971):373-386.

7. Eric H. Steele and James Jacobs, "A Theory of Prison Systems," *Crime and Delinquency* (April 1975):149-161.

8. See James Q. Wilson, "If Every Criminal Knew He Would Be Punished if Caught," *New York Times Magazine*, January 28, 1973, p. 53. © 1973 by The New York Times Company. Reprinted with permission.

9. Andrew Von Hirsch, *The Justice of Punishment*, report of the Committee for the Study of Incarceration (publication pending).

10. See, for example, Citizens' Inquiry Board on New York Parole and Criminal Justice, Inc., *Prison Without Walls* (New York: Citizens' Inquiry, 1974).

11. See Andrew Von Hirsch, *The Justice of Punishment*, report of the Committee for the Study of Incarceration (publication pending).

12. See Eric H. Steele and James Jacobs, "A Theory of Prison Systems," *Crime and Delinquency* 17 (October 1971):373-386.

13. John Conrad, "Corrections and Simple Justice," *Journal of Criminal Law and Criminology* (June 1973):217. Reprinted by special permission of the Journal of Criminal Law and Criminology, Copyright © 1973 by Northwestern University School of Law, Vol. 64, No. 2.

Part IV:
A Suggested Research
Agenda

7

What Should We Know?

Everything that has been said thus far leads to the conclusion that we don't know very much. We have a correctional system with certain objectives and certain practices. The system is evolving—general trends can be spotted, but the specifics can't be pinned down. Yet one premise of government is that change can be guided by planning, fueled by research.

What follows is an agenda of policy and research issues that must be faced within the next few years. First, a small set of critical issues are listed—issues that are so pressing that they must be addressed as soon as possible. This is followed by a longer enumeration of issues that are important, but either not so salient or not so policy-relevant as those in the first list. Finally, a list of key questions for consideration by state SPAs (State Planning Agencies) administering LEAA (Law Enforcement Assistance Administration) Safe Streets monies is included.

Key Policy Issues

Before we undertake the research outlined below, a set of working definitions and classifications should be developed, subject to revision as necessary. At a minimum the definitions should cover the following terms: recidivism, dangerousness, seriousness, incapacitation, community-based corrections, and deterrence (absolute and graded by "seriousness"). Classifications will be needed for types of offenses (they need not conform to existing statutory categories if other classifications would be more policy relevant—see pp. 69-74), and types of offenders by appropriate socioeconomic and demographic indicators, arrest and conviction records, and performance upon release in terms of employment and voluntary program participation.

Ideal information will never be available. Data on the rates of crime and types of offenders, etc., is inherently difficult to collect because all the incentives are wrong. Crooks aren't generally enthusiastic about supplying feature material on their activities, and law enforcement personnel have their own reasons for distortion. The result is that all the information that we would want to facilitate rational decision-making will never be available. At best we can get approximations.

Now a hypothetical: if there were a czar of correctional research and the czar were entrusted with ample—not endless, but ample—resources, what questions should appear at the top of his list?[a]

1. Recidivism. We simply don't know what the rearrest and reconviction rates are by type of offenders or by type of correctional disposition. Hence, definitive studies should be launched to fix recidivism rates by type of offender and offense. A common recidivism measure might be used in many studies but not in all. A common recidivism measure would disguise a lot of other probative variables. Recidivism rates are not simply a function of how well a correctional institution or system is doing, even if we control for the type of offender. Recidivism will vary with the intensity of police work, parole and probation, vigilance, the sophistication of law enforcement data collection systems, etc. Hence, while a common measure should be developed, a variety of recidivism measures, carefully defined and limited in application, will still have to be used where appropriate.

2. Crime Rates, Recidivism, and Exoffenders. Armed with hard recidivism data, the next inquiry should be how much crime of what type is attributable to exoffenders, by type of offender. In addition, we should ask how much crime of the total amount of crime, by type of offense, is committed by exoffenders, how long after release, by age and other sociodemographic indicators and by type of correctional disposition.

2a. Net Incapacitation Indexes. The combination of the first and second items in the list will make it possible to construct net incapacitation indexes for various correctional programs for various types of offenders. In other words, by matching hard information about recidivism with information about types of offenders, by types of offenses and by types of dispositions, we could create "net incapacitation indexes" that would tell us how much crime of various types the system prevents.

3. "Seriousness" Indexes. If we knew the recidivism rates for various classes of offenders, we could longitudinally trace (or do so retrospectively as well, if the data permit) career progressions of offenders in terms of seriousness. We could then determine whether any patterns of criminal behavior can be discovered for various types of offenders. This information would make the definition of recidivism a more useful and flexible resource.

4. "Dangerousness."[b] If we develop a category of dangerous offenders—this

---

[a]Completion of the research projects listed below may require a state of the art more sophisticated than is available. Because such may be the case, it is important to recognize that we do not presuppose that all the questions can be answered fully, but that first generation answers, or at least approximations, should be generated as soon as possible.

[b]The term is used here, as it is in the text, to include both the violent and the habitual offender.

is a policy, not a research, question—and if the category is not wholly based on a variety of indicators, then equipped with the data for items 1, 2, and 3, "culpability" indexes could be constructed based on past behavior and seriousness indexes. On the quantitative side, research could be commissioned to assess the impact on the correctional system of various definitions of "dangerousness"—that is, if only those who have committed six serious offenses are defined as dangerous, what is likely to be the impact on the prison population, the crime rate, the length of terms of other offenders?

If prediction technology is used instead of a test of culpability, much more research must be undertaken on the "causes" of crime, including the biological, psychophysiological, socioeconomic, and psychological. Then the data must be used to enhance the accuracy of predictive technology.[c]

5. A Typology of Offenders and Offenses. All the data accumulated in items 1 through 4 will fit into the larger typology discussed on pp. 70-71 and 72-73. Preparing such a typology and filling in as many of the cells will make it possible not only to assess the state of the art but to specify research projects to fill in additional cells.

6. The Role of the Prison. A determination of dangerousness presupposes a continued role for the prison (if it weren't already obvious that we would continue to use it). But questions of size, location, nature of program, and type of security system remain open. None of these questions has been resolved, and there is debate about all of them. Research should be done to relate the size, location, nature of program, and type of security of penal institutions with various correctional outcomes—including recidivism, deterrence, and incapacitation—and with the attitudes and preferences of inmates. This task is especially important if prison or prisonlike facilities are to be used in conjunction with community-based correctional programs either for short-term "shock" incarceration or for the housing of "furloughed" inmates participating in community programs.

6a. The Hierarchy of Prisons. A related question is the effects of degrees of punitiveness within a prison system. For example, is a maximum security prison essential to make the deterrent effect of the prison system credible? Comparative analyses in terms of deterrence, incapacitation, and recidivism could be made of correctional systems of varying mixes of facilities.

7. The Community. Presupposing the continued existence of the prison does not mean that the community will not serve as a site, perhaps even a principal site, for future correctional programs. But we know very little about the community. Consequently, the following inquiries should be undertaken:

---

[c]If predictive technology is to be used rather than a culpability test, given the current state of the art, it is presumed that additional research would enhance the precision of the technology and we would further presume that this greater precision would be desirable.

a. Each state SPA should be required to prepare "maps" of community resources in each appropriate community within the jurisdictions.
b. Case histories of exemplary community-based programs should be done so that "blueprints" are available for replication.[d]
c. Each state SPA should be required to furnish descriptive material on each community-based program of whatever type and vintage, together with any evaluative information available.
d. An examination should be made of the shift to the community in other social control systems—particularly mental health, because the shift to the community in mental health is likely to be accelerated by recent Supreme Court decisions.

8. Sentencing, Length of Sentence, and Correctional Outcomes. With a shift away from indeterminacy, both domestic and cross-cultural studies should be undertaken to ascertain the relationships, if any, among (a) the degree of indeterminacy, (b) the length of sentence, and (c) correctional outcomes in terms of recidivism, deterrence, and incapacitation.

8a. "Shock" Incarceration. Of particular importance because of current interest is the effect of short-term "shock" incarceration, again by type of offender and offense.

9. Reintegration and the Offender. If the proponents of reintegration are philosophically correct in their assertion that isolation severely compromises the offender's chances to "make it" once released, we need to know much more than we do about ways to integrate the correctional experience with the rest of our shared experience. This will require an examination of all those programs and practices, including those in other societies, that can be defined as "reintegrative." To the extent available, evaluative material should be stressed.

10. Impediments to Reform and the "Economy" of Corrections. To devise effective strategies for the implementation of reforms, more should be known about the impediments to reform. Chief among them are the vested economic interests in things as they are. Accordingly, the "economy" of corrections should be examined so that sources of resistance can be identified and dealt with.

These issues seem to be among the most determinative. Of course, there are other important ones. But those just mentioned were chosen not for their provocativeness but for their policy salience. More information about hidden crime, for example, would be useful, but it wouldn't or couldn't lead to the resolution of policy issues in the short run. The issues listed must be resolved in

---

[d]To the extent available, evaluation material always should be included.

the near future whether or not research results are available. Nevertheless, there are a host of other issues; what follows is an attempt to identify the most important among them.

Other Issues

The Context for Reform

1. We need to know more about the "limits" to change within corrections; the means by which change takes place; and the dynamics of the interaction among research, policy, and correctional practice.

2. Some survey research—as unreliable as the results often are—also should be undertaken to ascertain public attitudes toward reform. For example, community attitudes about different forms of community-based correctional programs could be assessed. Then, too, more should be known about public attitudes about crime in general.

3. The sources of change and resistance to change need some analysis. More specifically, we should find out more about the "key actors" to change: how they function, what the "diffusion" process is for innovative ideas, how ideas get contaminated and by whom, and what the sources of resistance to change are likely to be.

4. Exploration of what the change processes have been in other systems should be undertaken. For example, what were the mechanics of the swift and dramatic reductions in mental health censuses? And why was the reduction more thorough and swift in one state than in another?

5. Case studies could be done to assess why certain innovations—such as the reform of the juvenile detention systems in Massachusetts and Kentucky—seem to work in some places but not in others.

6. Finally, the impacts of research and policy initiatives on correctional practice should be examined.

Comparative Research[e]

There may be limits to the importability of practices from other cultures, particularly with respect to political and economic institutions. But there are things we can learn.

1. The first issue is the extent of social control. Why is it that most advanced western nations imprison fewer people than we do? But we should also identify other social control mechanisms at work in these societies. It may be that just as many people are subject to social control with more reliance placed on nonincarcerative mechanisms.

---

[e]This subject has been deemphasized in this project because of resource constraints.

2. Questions of size, location, and nature of the prison also loom large. There is evidence that penal institutions are smaller in other nations. What about location? What programs are available, and do they work? In Sweden, for example, some prisons are apparently organized around industrial operations, such as logging. What's the evidence on those prisons' effectiveness?

3. It may be that prisons are smaller in Scandinavia and the Netherlands. But what difference does it make? Are recidivism rates different than ours? Are there any other correctional outcomes to compare? Are the institutions more humane? Are the programs coercive or voluntary? Are they beneficial? Further, what uses are made of the community? Do other countries have more correctional programs in the community? And if so, what kinds of programs are used, and how successful are the programs?

4. What is the composition of offender populations in other societies, and what impact does it have on corrections and correctional outcomes? Who are the correctional officers, and how do they interact with prisoners?

5. What are the relationships between the correctional system and other systems of social control, such as mental health, education, and so on? What is the degree of transferability of the deviants? Are the various social control systems differently governed?

6. Perhaps the most fruitful area of inquiry is that of disposition options. What methods of correction, other than those we use in the United States, have been tried elsewhere? For example, what about the "relocation" of exoffenders? Have these methods worked? Would they be viable if we imported them?

The Definition of Crime

1. Not all deviant behavior is criminal behavior. What are the dynamics of the relationship between definitions of deviance and definitions of crime? Are there times when proportionately less (or more) behavior is defined as criminal than at other times? What is the proportion of predatory versus nonpredatory behavior classified as crime at any time? How permeable is the definition—that is, to what extent are deviant labels interchangeable?

2. A related question arises from the existence of social control mechanisms. To what extent does the supply of social control agents and mechanisms create a demand for their exercise? There is some evidence, for example, that diversion programs, aside from their merits, have not reduced or even held constant the amount of social control exercised, but rather, that they have increased it by approximately the number of persons subject to diversion (see pp. 100-103).

3. A final field of inquiry should be into relationships among the various social control programs. To what extent are deviants "transferred" from one system to another—for example, where does truancy end and delinquency begin? How many persons not fit to stand trial are subsequently reclassified as fit at a

later date? How many inmates, of what type, are "transferred" to mental health facilities, and vice versa? And, finally, assuming some stability in the number of persons subject to punishment, are there dynamic relationships among the various social control systems? For example, if the census drops in mental institutions, is the slack taken up by other systems, particularly corrections?

Reforms Within the Criminal Justice
System

Sentencing. A key premise for sentencing reform is that wide latitude in judicial discretion leads to intolerable inequities in disposition. A further premise is that the indeterminate sentence leads to abuses of discretion by correctional agencies, particularly parole boards. But there are some questions:

1. What is the relationship between indeterminacy and the length of sentence and, further, actual time served?

a. As sentences become more uniform through a diminishment of indeterminacy, are there compensating factors such as good time, early release privileges, and so on, which have the effect of restoring the discretion lost through statutory sentencing reforms?
b. What is the effect of plea-bargaining on sentences and sentencing practice?
c. What evidence is there that harsh and inequitable sentences are mitigated by parole authorities? Conversely, what evidence is there that parole authorities make original dispositions more severe?

2. Another pertinent inquiry is the impact of jury and judicial nullification: When the statutory requirements for sentencing are harsh, do juries and judges tend to mitigate the harshness of those sentences through their decisions? If so, to what extent? How much time is actually served when the statutory sentence is lengthy?

3. A related issue is sentencing innovation. What is the nature and extent of judicial inventiveness in sentencing? Anecdotal information is available about uniquely tailored sentences meted out by judges, but how much of this is there, and how do the outcomes compare with more conventional correctional dispositions?

4. As to corrections:

a. What are the relationships, if any, between indeterminacy and correctional practice?
b. Is the emphasis in terms of resource allocation on rehabilitation greater when indeterminacy is greater?
c. Do recidivism rates vary at all with indeterminacy? With longer or shorter sentences?

d. And, most important, do correctional outcome rates vary with the type of disposition—incarceration versus early parole versus deferred parole, and so on?

Plea-Bargaining.

1. How widespread is it? Data are tossed around about the high percentage of dispositions based on plea-bargaining in large urban jurisdictions, but what about Keokuk, Iowa? What is the overall percentage of cases disposed of through plea-bargaining jurisdiction to jurisdiction?
2. In addition, what is the variation in techniques—in how many jurisdictions is a record kept, or is the defendant permitted to participate, and so forth?
3. Is there any evidence that the number and severity of charges pressed by the prosecutor are associated with expectations that plea-bargaining will ensue?
4. Perhaps a more important inquiry would be addressed to the outcome of the disposition: What is the variation between sentences received for like offenses by matched groups of offenders based on the nature of disposition—a guilty plea without bargaining, plea-bargaining, and trial and conviction?
5. Even more specifically, what evidence is there that offenders eschewing plea-bargaining are given discriminatorily severe sentences for like offenses?
6. Finally, are there some offenses for which plea-bargaining is used more frequently than others, or is plea-bargaining fairly uniform across offenses from jurisdiction to jurisdiction? Controlling for statutory maxima and minima, what is the variation in sentences among jurisdictions when plea-bargaining is used?

Decriminalization.

1. First an historical perspective: What have been the ramifications of decriminalization in the past? More work needs to be done on Kai Erikson's hypothesis: have new offenses been created to take the place of those that are decriminalized? It is also argued that as behaviors are decriminalized, the load on the criminal justice system will lighten, and in time, the flow of offenders to the correctional system will correspondingly dry up. Is there any further historical evidence for this phenomenon?
2. There are other questions:

a. Will decriminalization result in less, the same, or more social control? If the same or more, will corrections have fewer people to work with in the future? That is, if the "slots" occupied by offenders without victims are emptied by decriminalization, will these slots be filled by someone else, either for an offense left on the books or for a new offense newly legislated?
b. If the "target" populations for criminal control change—if the number of

slots stays fixed but if the slots are filled by different people—what kind of people are they likely to be, and what are the resulting implications for corrections?

c. If decriminalization does result in less social control, even if only for a short time, what are the implications for corrections? Will fewer "referrals" be made? Will judges fill the gap by imposing longer sentences for more people? If fewer people show up at corrections' door, will the system naturally try to hang on to them longer to keep itself busy?

d. Will there be any impact on correctional outcomes? Are offenders who committed so-called victimless crimes more or less likely to recidivate than other offenders? If so, are there differences in terms of outcomes among the various types of offenders who will no longer be processed through the criminal justice system? For example, do hookers recidivate more than gamblers?

The "Dangerous/Habitual" Offender.

1. How much of total crime is committed by people who have committed one, three, five, ten crimes before? Are there patterns of habituation? Do repeaters diversify or confine their activities to one kind of crime or to a "family" of crimes?

2. How much of the dangerous/habitual offender's activity is violent? What kind? Are there any sociodemographic peculiarities about such offenders?

3. Is there any evidence that different correctional modalities, the prison, probation, diversion, and so forth influence rearrest rates among those who are otherwise classified as dangerous/habitual criminals? or as to the various types of dangerous/habitual offender—for example, thief versus rapist? More important perhaps, have any programs had a demonstrable impact on such offenders?

Seriousness. We must know more about the patterns of crime of selected offender groups and about aggregate statistical trends in seriousness of crime commission.[f]

---

[f]A sound basis for measuring seriousness is the seriousness score developed by Thorstein Sellin and Marvin Wolfgang, described in *The Measurement of Delinquency* (New York: John Wiley & Sons, 1964), especially Chapters 15-17. Essentially they attempted to generate a scale of the seriousness of various criminal offenses by comparing the responses of different representative samples of the population to descriptions of criminal behavior. The methodology for converting these responses into a numerical scale is quite complex, but the end result was that there was substantial consistency among the various groups. The numerical scores used in Marvin Wolfgang, Thorstein Sellin and Franco Ferracuti, *Delinquency in a Birth Cohort* (Chicago: University of Chicago Press, 1972), fn. 132, were based on the seriousness scales developed in the earlier work and allowed the authors to compare *levels* of crime, rather than just gross numbers of offenses. For a recent examination of the "state of the art" in developing and using seriousness scores, see "Symposium on the Measurement of Delinquency," *Journal of Criminal Law and Criminology* 66 (June 1975):173-221.

Diversion.

1. There are two central issues: First, the impact diversion has on the "traditional" system, if any—for example, are the slots vacated by diversionees occupied by others?—and second, the "outcomes" of diversion in terms of recidivism (or any other measure) vis-à-vis traditional correctional outcomes. More specifically, do any "packages" of diversion programs seem to be more effective than others?

2. Case history research would seem to be particularly pertinent. For example, has any diversion program had a demonstrable impact on the traditional system with which it coexists—that is, any traditional systems incorporated diversion programs and/or practices as a result of evaluation of diversion? If so, what kinds of programs and what types of practices?

Administrative Efficiency. There are a number of linked reforms under this rubric, but one in particular—the speedy trial—may have a direct bearing on corrections. A number of legislative proposals (some have been enacted) would require a trial, or other disposition, within X number of days of the issuance of formal charges. Assuming that the speed of punishment (along with its certainty) enhances the deterrent effect of the criminal sanction, what evidence is there, by comparing jurisdictions, that speedier dispositions have either a more powerful specific or general deterrent effect?

Criminology and the Causes of Crime

1. There is no simple "cause" of crime, but rather a cluster of causes, including the social, economic, psychological, biological, and psychophysiological. This melange must be analyzed and the separate determinants weighted to the extent possible.[g]

2. If crime is in part attributable to social and environmental conditions, to what extent?

a. What are the social and environmental factors that are presumably involved?

b. Once a set has been developed, what is the relative weighting to be given to each such factor?

c. Is there a "critical mass" of factors that can be said to increase significantly the likelihood of criminal conduct on the part of individuals exposed to those conditions?

---

[g]No matter how influential social and environmental conditions are in the crime rate, the function is far from linear (X will always commit Z if exposed to social and environmental conditions A, B, and C). And until all crime can be accounted for by looking at A, B, and C—if X and Y are similarly situated, both must do Z—the individual must be examined also.

d. What evidence is there that alteration in the "underlying" causes of crime introduces like alteration in the amount of criminal behavior? For example, with more unemployment, do the rates of certain crimes increase correspondingly?

3. Because not all similarly situated people engage in criminal conduct, what individual factors are influential in either motivating or deterring criminal conduct, and what are the dynamics of the interaction of social and individual variables?

4. Other issues related to the causation of crime require attention:

a. How widespread is senseless violence? Is its incidence increasing, controlling for population, and why?
b. To what extent is crime becoming more "collective," and individual responsibility becoming harder to fix?
c. What peculiar factors lead to a disproportionate amount of crime among the young?
d. Is there a marked increase in the amount of crime committed by women? If so, do any particular causative factors contribute to the increase?

The Functions of Punishment

Social Defense/Incapacitation. Are there relationships among the length of sentence, rearrest rates, and extent and nature of subsequent offenses? (It would then be possible to construct a calculus of "protection" as a function of length of incapacitation in relation to subsequent criminal behavior, weighted for damage done.)

Retribution. What evidence is there, based on survey research, about the parameters of punishment that society will accept? There is survey data on the death penalty, but what about other offenses?[h]

Deterrence.[i] Concerning both general and special deterrence, the important questions are:[j]

---

[h]If "just deserts" function, as the Committee for the Study of Incarceration argues, as both the floor and ceiling to punishment, where is the data on which to base floor and ceiling measurements to be obtained? In large measure, because survey research is so problematic, the only test of the public's acceptance is ultimately a "market" test: If certain limits are set, what will the public's reaction be, if any? But the public's reaction in turn will be closely related to its perception of the "outcomes" of corrections in terms of recidivism, which, in turn, is a function of the deterrent capacity of the correctional experience. This, then, is an example of the interrelatedness of correctional purposes. It also demonstrates that if retribution is articulated as an objective, social defense notions are necessarily involved.

[i]I can't do much better in itemizing the research agenda for examination of deterrence than Zimring and Hawkins have already done (*Deterrence*; Chicago: University of Chicago Press, 1973). But their list is lengthy. The following are some key questions out of the larger set.

[j]Once again, I stress that these are not necessarily research projects themselves, but rather questions that can be broken down into researchable bits.

1. What is the relative deterrent effect of the various correctional modalities—incarceration, probation, diversion, fines, restitution, combinations of these?
2. What is the relative deterrent effect of those modalities, offense by offense?
3. What is the relative deterrent effect of those correctional modalities on different types of offenders as defined by sociodemographic variables?
4. What are the marginal deterrent effects of the length and nature of the disposition as to: (a) further offenses in general; (b) specific offenses; and (c) different types of offenders.

Each of these sets of questions can be further conceptualized to test the effects of (1) the nature of the threat; (2) the communication of the threat; (3) the perception of threat; and (4) the "reaction" to the threat.

As to general deterrence, the key issues, in descending order of specificity, are:

1. What is the general deterrent effect of the penal system?
2. What is the general deterrent effect of specific modalities of corrections, including prison, probation, diversion, fine, restitution, and others?
3. What is the relative deterrent effect of these modalities, offense by offense?
4. What is the relative deterrent effect of these correctional modalities on different types of offenders as defined by sociodemographic variables?

A last area of inquiry should address, to the extent possible, the deterrent impact of deeply embedded mores and cultural constructs. The inhibitions that curb antisocial behavior may derive only rarely from the punishment of others.

Rehabilitation.

1. How do we account for individual prison success and aggregate prison failure? Are some rehabilitative programs successful? If so, do they have any common features?

2. On the other hand, if it is true that "nothing works"—as it is often asserted—it is still important to try to find out why. The demise of rehabilitation as a "purpose" for punishment does not mean that programs will not continue to be provided. Consequently, given the resources consumed in doing the job, we should investigate the reasons for its failure:

a. Were, for example, the resources expended inadequate to truly test the effectiveness of treatment?
b. Is the prison as an institution so inconducive to treatment, either voluntary or "coerced," that it simply cannot work?

c. Is there any variability in result depending on the correctional modality—in particular, the prison, probation, and diversion?
d. Does some treatment appear to be more effective with certain types of offenders, or are all offenders equally unaffected?
e. What was the relationship, if any, between the length of sentence and treatment outcome, and what were the relative outcomes of treatment in the prison and the same treatment with free world subjects?

3. Some reintegration advocates argue that the idea of rehabilitation is still viable if coercion can be eliminated from the treatment process. But can it?

a. What is the evidence that it contaminates the treatment effort?
b. Are there any differences in outcome when coercion is controlled, to the extent possible, as an independent variable, both in the correctional setting and outside it?
c. Is there any evidence that treatment outcomes vary with the degree to which parole authorities take such outcomes into consideration?
d. As a way of generating some data with which to make comparisons, what is the evidence about the outcomes of rehabilitation in other settings? That is, how effective are remedial education, job training, and various therapeutic programs by type of offense and offender?

4. A final inquiry should be directed towards various rehabilitation program elements. Rehabilitation is not a single tool, but a congeries of programs with the same purpose. Each distinguishable element—education, job training, counseling, and so forth—should be examined independently.

Correctional Practice

1. Survey research should be conducted to ascertain inmate attitudes about various correctional practices.
2. Because so much of the fuel in the prisoners' movement in corrections has been the result of legal activism of prisoners and prisoners' movements, research should be undertaken on the actual impact of the prison legal reform movement. It is often argued that new rights and privileges have accrued to the prisoner as a result of litigation. But legal initiatives can be counterintuitive. Consequently, case studies should be undertaken, based on apparent changes in correctional practice due to the impress of legal decisions to ascertain what the long-term benefits and/or long-term costs have been.
3. Prison overcrowding is alleged and should be studied. Specifically, census data should be compiled from the various jurisdictions over time, vis-à-vis available beds, and then should be evaluated; the data may correlate with recidivism and other correctional outcome measures.

4. One of the linchpins of the reintegration movement is that treatment can be provided without coercion. Among other things, the implications of a thorough assessment of coercion should be drawn out as to reintegration programs, community-based corrections, and so forth. More specifically, an examination should be made of the effects of various types of coercion (rules, incentives, threats, penalties, etc.) on various types of correctional programming; for example, does an incentive "work" with vocational training but fail with respect to work release?

5. Finally, studies should be undertaken to ascertain the amount of crime that occurs within the prison.

Correctional Reform

1. The major area in need of research is community-based corrections. The issues include:

a. If community, whose community? Not all offenders come from the city or the same part of any city.

b. Should the community be the same community—when at least some offenders ostensibly got into trouble in that same community?

c. Because not everybody can be returned to his or her community, what will substitute for the social links abruptly severed by rural incarceration but not so obviously available in the new community?

d. How widespread is the movement?[k]

e. What new technology, if any, is necessary to ensure security in the community? What kind of surveillance systems will be developed, if any, and what are the implications for offender privacy and dignity?

f. What are the successful prototype programs, and what, if any, is their "success" in terms of rehabilitation, recidivism, or whatever measure is used?[l]

2. What is the optimal size for the prison, based on a comparative analysis of prisons in other countries in relation to correctional outcomes? A similar analysis might focus on prison location because it is now widely argued that corrections should take place in the city rather than rural areas.[m]

---

[k]A 1972 survey shows that only a little over 4000 offenders were participating in what could be called community-based programs out of a total offender population of roughly 500,000. See Bertram S. Griggs and Gary R. McCone, "Community-based Correctional Programs: A Survey and Analysis," *Federal Probation* 36 (June 1972):8.

[l]There is some research: the "Warren" studies undertaken in California purported to show better success in the community. But as Martinson points out, the "reason" for the results was preferential treatment of the experimentals by the probation officers. See Robert Martinson, "What Works?—Questions and Answers About Prison Reform," *The Public Interest* 35 (Spring 1974):22-54.

[m]The research should not consider optimality of size and location wholly in terms of recidivism but also in terms of other measures of correctional success to the extent to which they can be developed.

3. To date, the activities of the major reform commissions in the criminal justice field have produced mounds of material with a substantial number of recommendations. A retrospective assessment should be done to ascertain the degree of implementation, if any, of each recommendation concerning corrections. Not only would this tell us something about the impact of major commissions, it also would provide an opportunity analyzing the major impediments and restraints to reform.

4. Economic analysis has contributed one of the most promising bodies of contemporary research in corrections. Among the key questions to be examined are:

a. the degree to which crime "pays"; a calculus should be constructed to assess the relative benefits of engagement in crime versus the risk of apprehension

b. an analysis of the information available to the average offender prior to or at the point of committing a crime to assess the limits of the deterrent effect

c. analysis of the costs and benefits of community-based corrections in its various modalities, traditional correctional practice, and diversion programs.

5. The related but distinguishable issues of the fine, restitution, and victim compensation need far more work. At a minimum, we need to know more about:

a. the "taxing" effect on legitimate activity of the fine and restitution

b. the deterrent and incapacitative effects of the fine and restitution

c. the relationships among the fine, restitution, and victim-compensation schemes.

6. Research should also be undertaken to assess the implications for social control of a shift to the community in corrections. As pointed out, if security is to be maintained in the community, new schemes of security will have to be developed. Research should seek to ascertain the extent to which surveillance technology is now available or is likely to be available in the future, and the extent to which that technology can be easily and efficiently deployed in correctional settings.

Key Issues for State SPAs

Much of the correctional R&D dollar is spent by state SPAs administering the LEAA Safe Streets block grant funds, although basic research is not generally within their authority. Many of these agencies lack a sufficiently clear vision of how to spend their money. Many of the topics suggested here require basic research of a sort that only NILECJ (National Institute of Law Enforcement and Criminal Justice) or private foundations can support. But there are R&D projects and evaluation efforts that state SPAs can and should support. Some of the more crucial are:

1. A descriptive and evaluative assessment of existing community-based correctional programs
2. Preparation of "maps" of community correctional resources, including specific opportunities for placement
3. Evaluation of correctional programs in terms of their outcomes—that is, impact on recidivism rates (a common definition should be used by all SPAs), deterrent effects, and net incapacitation effects
4. Diversion programs. Because they are locally operated, they are ideal subjects for state and/or regional SPAs. The same is true for plea-bargaining. In each case the questions posed on pp. 91 and 95 should be considered.
5. Community correctional security measures, a locally based subject. What security measures are actually used in community-based correctional programs, including probation, halfway houses, and diversion? How effective are they?
6. Exploration of "private" correctional resources (discussed on p. 100), which also could be undertaken at the local level. These resources should also be included in no. 2 above.
7. Data correlating (a) indeterminacy of sentence with (b) length of sentence and time actually served, and (c) correctional outcomes. Each state SPA should be required to generate these data.
8. Information about existing detention facilities in the community to determine their convertibility into facilities in support of new community-based corrections programs and their current usage compatible with such purposes. Because the prison still may be used in community-based corrections as a resource center and/or short-term lockup, state SPAs should be required to furnish this information.

Part V:
Epilogue: The Politics
of Change

8

Is Change Likely?

This book has raised more questions than it has answered. That has been its purpose. Yet even if we did know more, we still would face formidable difficulties in introducing change into the system. Part of the reason is that we aren't very sure about the changes that should be made. But beyond this, the resistance to change of any kind remains strong.

The problem may be political.

Because corrections has no constituency, it lacks political clout, and therefore it is starved for the resources it needs to do the job. But this really is a limited point. Undoubtedly, corrections stands far back in the line for its share of public resources. But what would it do with more money? It could retain more competent staff, enact correctional programs, and refurbish detention facilities. These are important considerations. But beyond that, because corrections has no clear mission in view, the consumption of additional resources would be a case of having eyes bigger than its stomach.

Another argument is that the resistance to change arises simply because the public won't tolerate changes it perceives as "soft-hearted." In other words, to the general public, the crook doesn't deserve anything more than a cell, a modicum of personal safety, and a balanced diet. Of course, there is some validity to this argument. The public has hardly appeared charitable in its attitude towards the offender, particularly the exoffender. As tired as we are of hearing about it, it is nevertheless true that we are harsh in our treatment of the offender, and that part of our harshness stems from our assumption that the offender is somehow different, even defective.

There are at least two other major impediments to change, one quite straightforward and the other more subtle. The first is that as long as offenders exploit their victims, for whatever reasons, the public will remain unmoved by pleas for reform that offer no solace for the victim. And it is true that few correctional reforms include such a plan, nor could they if they are realistic about the role of corrections in crime control.

The second reason is that there is no clear charter for the reformation. Corrections is hardly monolithic; it is tugged and pulled by interest groups with different goals. These varying and often conflicting interests have not achieved any consensus on the direction of change. They remain at the bargaining table. What are the interests and what are the issues?

Perspectives on Change

Inmates

No Gallup or Harris polls have been taken to reflect inmate attitudes. Most of what we know about the inmate has been based on what has been written by exinmates, or on what is occasionally pirated out of the prisons. Unfortunately, the information we get may be skewed. The articulate inmate—the one who makes his or her views known—may not be representative.

One source of information about inmate attitudes is Jonathan Casper's study of the "consumer" perspective in criminal justice.[1] Casper interviewed seventy persons, including parolees, probationers, and inmates. In assessing their views, he found that "consumers" had values that were remarkably consistent with the establishment's. Most inmates wanted to change themselves to conform and were willing to accept punishment in a system that they perceived as just. As a result, Casper concludes:

If the system is to teach [the offender] that there are other ways to live, that he can deal with individuals in ways other than exploitation, pressuring, and conning, then it should convince him that he is not being treated in these ways. This is not to say that if the men were treated differently within the criminal justice system—if they got the feeling that they were being dealt with as individuals by others who cared about them and their problems—that suddenly and miraculously they would "go straight" and turn into happy, productive, law-abiding citizens. The economic and social conditions of their lives on the street and their psychological characteristics are also crucial determinants of their behavior. But it is to say that if we are concerned about criminal behavior and about reducing it, one facet of institutional reform aimed at achieving this goal should concentrate upon the quality of the administration of justice.[2]

Casper's sample was small. It may not be representative; there may not be a coherent "inmate" perspective. But even if there isn't, there are some fairly well-known grievances.

First, there is raw hostility and anger. Prisoner hostility can be expected, Karl Menninger observes, when the prisoner is "herded about by men half afraid and half contemptuous of him, towards whom all offenders early learn to present a steadfast attitude of hostility."[3] This "cattle car" attitude of the keepers exacerbates the frustration of the powerless drift in which the inmate exists.[a] Despite lengthy lists of codes and regulations, the amount of discretion left to supervisors remains substantial; they have countless opportunities to demean the inmate. And lawlessness directed towards an inmate corrodes inmate's confidence and renders him or her more lawless in turn.

---

[a] As one exinmate puts it, "Dr. Victor Frankl, the Viennese psychoanalyst who lived through years in Nazi prison camps, including Buchenwald, has said the most terrible thing he experienced was not starving or freezing or being dehumanized. The most terrible thing was not knowing how long it would last." Edward Bunker, "Getting 'Insight' from Behind Bars," *Los Angeles Times*, March 25, 1975, Part IV, p. 5.

Inmates also have expressed deep disagreement with some specifics of prison life. Targets have included parole practices, racism, the indeterminate sentence, and the length of sentences.

The racism issue is at once simple and complex.[b] There is little doubt that systematic racial prejudice has disproportionately populated the prison with blacks and other racial minorities, including Mexican-Americans and Amerindians. A recent study is illustrative: "There is a significant absolute disparity between the sentences received by black offenders and those received by white offenders. . . . Careful analysis of the data failed to reveal any general factor which would account for the disparity other than race."[4] These "institutional" forms of racism have been documented as well by the New York State Attica Commission and by the Federal Commission on Civil Rights.[5]

Beyond institutional racism, there is the effort of correctional personnel to "divide and conquer" the inmate population by occasionally blatant appeals to racism. As one inmate describes it:

The guards here stir up prisoners. There hasn't been a serious race riot here now for over a year and things were going pretty smoothly, but the guards started spreading rumors that the cells were going to be integrated just to make things tense. No one wants that. The whites do not want to live with the blacks, and the blacks don't want to live with the whites. The guards come up to a white prisoner in his cell and say, "How would you like a black cell partner?" That gets the white prisoner up tight and increases the tensions in the prison.[6]

Inmates don't object to parole; they object to parole discretion. Parole decisions appear to be made without criteria, or if criteria are used they are either unknown or unfairly applied. Moreover, many prisoners feel that parole standards are corrupting; they are based on unrealistic expectations irrelevant to postrelease behavior. David Fogel includes the following inmate comment: "If they ask if this yellow wall is blue, I'll say, of course, it's blue. I'll say anything they want me to say if they're getting ready to let me go."[7] As pointed out in Chapter 5, a large amount of this discretion exercised at parole is the result of indeterminacy in sentencing. But the opposition of inmates to indeterminacy goes beyond the parole process. Inmates who oppose indeterminacy do so at least in part because it has led to lengthier sentences.[8,c] Many inmates who support a return to fixed sentences probably do so because they expect shorter sentences to result.

A remaining phenomenon is the political prisoner.[9] It has always been argued that some individuals are swept up by the criminal justice broom for political reasons. But today some prisoners and many prisoner groups take the position that whole classes of prisoners—blacks, Chicanos, Black Muslims, the poor, draft resisters—have been the target of systematic repression through the use of the

---

[b]The issue is discussed in more detail in Chapter 5, pp. 86-89.

[c]Of course, other factors influence sentence length, including increased use of probation instead of incarceration for lesser offenses; but the impact of indeterminacy is substantial.

criminal sanction. The theory finds support in the radical wing of the "inter-actionist" school of criminology. The data are provocative as well. As Table 5-2 (p. 88) illustrates, prison is a much more likely habitat for blacks than for whites. Some of the effects of politicization on corrections are becoming clear. First, by forming groups to oppose penal policies, inmates not only strengthen their own position through their solidarity, but they also align themselves with interest groups outside the prison, hence maximizing their leverage. This certainly has been the case with some black inmate organizations, particularly the Black Muslims. Second, treatment programs—or for that matter, many "self-help" programs—may be compromised because inmates, believing their imprisonments to have been politically motivated, will not believe that "help" is needed. Third and finally, the prison experience, which has reformation of the inmate as at least one of its purposes, may be transformed instead into a radicalizing experience for the inmate exposed to the argument that his or her crime wasn't a crime at all, but rather a political act.

The prison is a "total institution," to use Erving Goffman's phrase,[10] and any attempt to shift power from the keepers to the kept will be awesomely resisted.[11] Attica is a sufficient example.[12] As a result, politicization among prisoners is nearly anathema to prison administrators. As Fogel points out, there has been more resistance to prisoner rights litigation over the issue of inmate political organization within the prison than on any other issue.[13]

One of the ways inmates, exoffenders, and other sympathizers express their views is through litigation. Recent years have seen a landslide of lawsuits dealing with prisoners' rights. Rights to religious expression, association, and free speech have been enlarged. Disciplinary actions and related administrative actions affecting inmate privileges have been circumscribed. And many brutal prison practices adjudged to be "cruel and unusual" have been halted.[14] Most of these developments are recited in Goldfarb and Singer, *After Conviction.*[15] As a result of this activity, prisoners have gained a lot of ground. And there are no signs that litigation will abate. Among other things, increasing inmate organization has fomented litigation as a means of vindicating rights of association and expression. As more suits are tried, more lawyers and more judges have become acclimated to the geography of prisoners' rights and remedies.

There is a natural limit, however. Litigation is a time-consuming, episodic affair. Broad and lasting change is difficult to achieve when litigation is the sole weapon. Litigation probably will continue to be used as a "prod" to adminis-trative and legislative action, but it is unlikely to introduce sweeping change.

The point is this, then: In the past, prisoners lacked effective political tools to influence the larger debate about the aims and purposes of corrections. That is not the case today. Today inmates and inmate groups, particularly those who understand the political use of media, have more influence. Yet ultimately, inmates will necessarily remain weak in the political arena. They lack an effective constituency; they can't vote once they get out; and many who get out quickly sever any ties with other inmates and inmate organizations for fear of social disapproval.

Supervisors and Guards

If there is no unity of view among inmates, it is hardly more apparent among correctional supervisory personnel. First, the views of correctional department heads, wardens, and guards differ on crucial issues, mostly because they occupy different positions in the prison hierarchy. But there may also be some constants. The need for security is preeminent; almost all ideological differences are submerged in this purpose. Charles McKendrick, one of the few correctional practitioners who has written on the subject, makes it clear:

For centuries, prisons have been constructed with a single objective, that of security. In a sense, each new prison was an experiment in construction. Whenever an escape occurred, some effort was made to strengthen the physical plant. A wall was constructed, more windows were barred, or perhaps a new position was created and a guard delegated to eliminate the weak point. The modern prison plant has developed as a result of earlier failures and, expensive as it may be, the modern walled prison is sufficiently secure to prevent escape, provided that neither the personnel nor the procedures of operation are in themselves defective.[16]

Change, then, any change, is likely to be opposed just because it rearranges the parts; and until the parts are once more locked into place, security is compromised.[17] This is probably why the rehabilitation movement was resisted among custodial personnel; the very presence of rehabilitators loosens security. Allen L. Ault, Commissioner of Corrections in Georgia, argues ". . . that the majority of the staff are reinforced for keeping things secure . . . they keep their jobs if there are few escapes and if not too many inmates or staff members get killed. Treatment, on the other hand, implies that you must take inmates out of secure areas. . . ."[18]

A final "constant" may be estrangement. Supervisory personnel are often from different sociodemographic strata than the inmates. Although he has possibly overstated it, Herman Schwartz characterizes guards this way: "These people usually have no understanding or sympathy for these strange urban groups, with their unfamiliar and often immoral lifestyles, with their demands and their resentments."[19]

There have been a few studies of supervisory attitudes. Joseph W. Eaton found that among all categories of personnel in corrections, only a majority of guards were opposed to rehabilitation as a principal purpose of corrections.[20] In another study, the findings of Gene C. Kassebaum, David A. Ward, and Daniel M. Wilner[21] corroborated Eaton's work. Supervisory attitudes are not monolithic; there are differences, but to Eaton they are matters of degree:

Differences in outlook between the more reform and the more punishment oriented correction officials were a matter of degree rather than of mutually exclusive convictions. Proponents of both penal philosophies were agreed upon the ultimate objective of correctional work: the attainment of maximum social control over deviance. No society can survive if the laws and morals can be violated without constraints.[22]

So as long as the needs for security remain dominant in corrections, correctional officers are likely to oppose any innovation of any ideological stripe that "rocks the boat."

Politicians and Policy-Makers

Any reorientation in corrections will confront some political boundaries. First, as long as there is "fear in the streets," most politicians will continue to call for measures to deal with it.[23] This means that there will be pitched resistance to reducing both the number of inmates and the length of sentence. And this will occur even though such measures have a dubious association with the level of crime in a community. In addition, while community-based corrections may receive some spirited rhetorical support, any spirited attempt to establish a program in a politician's backyard will generally be opposed: community-based corrections may be a good idea—but in someone else's district.

In the future, politicians probably will express more sympathy for the victim. In fact, they are already doing so. A cursory review of the articles and even newspaper accounts dealing with corrections and criminal justice reveals a renewed interest in the victim.[d] If this sympathy is translated into compensation, it will undoubtedly mean fewer resources for corrections, which is already starved by legislatures because of its lack of a powerful constituency.

The political reaction to the shift away from rehabilitation is hard to call. On one hand, a return to fixed terms and the philosophies of punishment to fit the crime and retribution should muster some public support, but the "lag" problem referred to earlier may cloud the issue—just as the public has begun to absorb rehabilitation rhetoric, it will be asked to shift its fidelity to a new program with new objectives.[e]

In sum, as long as corrections remains a backwater issue in politics (and as long as there is no rash of Attica-like prison riots) the political response to corrections and correctional reform can be expected to continue.

---

[d]See, for example, "The Christeen Gibsons Need Tears Too," by James J. Kilpatrick, in the *Los Angeles Times*, May 5, 1975. Kilpatrick recounts how Christeen Gibson, age 56, was robbed and badly beaten while minding a grocery store. She was permanently injured and couldn't work again. The offender was caught and imprisoned at a cost of $3600 per year. But, Kilpatrick asks, what about Christeen Gibson?

[e]Just such a shift is being made in Illinois with the implementation of the Walker Commission Report.

The Research Community

Researchers can exert a powerful influence on the debate about corrections. The renascence of "deterrence" as a viable concept owes much to some dogged investigators who thought the issues were worth exploring. And the erosion of the rehabilitation model, now so visible, is due in large measure to the torrents of criticism launched at it by some researchers.[24] But some problems remain.

The research community is in no sense a community—there is no unity of purpose among researchers, nor need there be. But in the anarchy that ensues, the research that is done may not focus on the most pressing problems. An opportunity exists to systematize some research through the LEAA program, particularly through the National Institute of Law Enforcement and Criminal Justice. Yet to date there isn't much evidence that coherence has resulted.

An additional problem is that many researchers have remained aloof from the practical problems of corrections. Of course, this is true in virtually every social problem area. Robert Martinson, in an unpublished manuscript,[f] scornfully assails researchers, particularly criminologists, for their failure to look at the "real" issues—such as the existence of crime and the public reaction to it in areas like the twentieth precinct of New York City, where Martinson lives.

The final problem that plagues research, not only in corrections, is the failure of researchers to sensitize themselves to the policy process. Decisions are constantly made, at both state and federal levels, about the correctional enterprise. Most of the time, these decisions are made without the benefit of sound research results. This link must be improved if research is to have a greater impact on the formulation of policy.

Judges and Lawyers

The role of judges has been more sensitive with the advent of the indeterminate sentence. Their role has been easier in one sense because wide tolerances in sentencing discretion afford them the opportunity to escape the responsibility of gauging the sentence to the offender. But at the same time, the judiciary cannot escape any responsibility for the abuses of the indeterminate sentence and certainly should be pilloried for the inexplicable diversity of sentences within the bounds of indeterminacy. Recently a number of commentators, including some judges, have drawn attention to the extreme, sometimes irrational diversity in judicial sentencing.

The judiciary isn't altogether insensitive to this problem. A recent book by

---

[f]Robert Martinson, "Toward a New Criminology" (unpublished manuscript 1975), especially Part II, "A View from the Twentieth Precinct." One of the issues Martinson puts high on his list is an examination of what he calls "life cycle" damage: because so much crime is age-specific, what can we learn about the nature of the "damage" done to those who commit crimes at crucial times in their lives, particularly adolescence?

Marvin E. Frankel, *Criminal Sentences*, couples an enlightened attitude with some concrete recommendations.[25] Sentencing is also a target of the Committee for the Study of Incarceration.[26] As a result, some reformulation of judicial sentencing is to be expected. In all likelihood, sentencing discretion will be limited—and if so, this development should calibrate with the larger effort to reduce statutory indeterminacy.

The Federal Role

With the passage of the Safe Streets legislation in 1968, the federal government announced its intention to solve the crisis of crime by doing what it does best: spending money. In 1969 the budget of LEAA, the agency designated to spend the money, was $63 million. In 1974 the budget had risen to $880 million. And although slight budget cuts have been proposed for the next fiscal year, the program shows no real signs of slowing down. And this is likely to be the result even though tossing millions of dollars around hasn't had any measurable effect on crime rates.[g] To some the reason is that most of the monies have been foolishly spent on elaborate policing technology, to the neglect of programs designed either to ameliorate social and economic conditions or to develop crime prevention measures.[27] To others, although possibly they agree that spending priorities have been out of whack, the problem is that crime is such an institutional feature of contemporary life that to expect major crime reductions is unrealistic.

These questions, of course, are very complex. Even if a substantial amount of the money spent on crime control is foolishly spent, it doesn't mean that spending less wouldn't make any difference. It may be necessary to pump great sums of money into the system just to hold the crime rate where it is. In any event, given the volatile nature of the crime issue, it is unlikely that expenditures on its control will dip much in the near future.

Beyond the expenditure of funds, the federal government also can influence the evolution of corrections by undertaking or commissioning the research necessary to chart the course. This requires the specification of objectives and research needs and the capacity to develop a plan and stick to it. Leaving aside whether this kind of centralization is desirable, government may not be capable of that kind of sustained action. Of course, the alternative is perpetuating the balkanization of the crime control effort that has always characterized the system. There is a real tradeoff here. The local control of the war on crime may be the best route, but reliance on local control introduces inequities and unevenness in both the content and enforcement of the law. Thus far the choice has been local control, with steadily increasing federal fiscal support. And given the fears about a national police force, local control probably will continue.

---

[g]Lately the press has pounced on this statistical "quirk."

The "Economy" of Corrections

One reason we have too much hospitalization is that we have too many hospital beds—supply can create demand. This is demonstrably so in medicine and to a somewhat lesser degree in the law. But it may also be true of cells, guards, and probation and parole officers. The prison is a business, as is probation and parole. Annually $2.7 billion are turned over in the corrections industry. The state and federal systems employ 190,000 people. In addition, the Federal Bureau's prison industry alone generates $58 million.[28] Finally, the federal government and the states combined spend an undetermined sum on research and program development related to corrections. This isn't exactly Exxon, but it's not insignificant. And in many small towns dotted across the United States, the prison is the staple industry—shut the prison down and you shut down the town.

Next, add to these cash flows the swarm of researchers, therapists, and bureaucrats who are sustained by the correctional business. None of these people, nor those directly employed in penal work, would be overjoyed if the system were jettisoned. As a result, it is argued, often by offenders and exoffenders, that the system managers are the real blocks to reform. Any reform that might reduce the size of the system is likely to be opposed. Of course, this is true in almost any labor-intensive field—it's what featherbedding is all about. Some proof of the accusation is furnished by recent experience. In 1972, when the Massachusetts State Department of Institutions sought to bulldoze the juvenile detention facilities, nothing could be done until the jobs of those affected had been secured elsewhere.[29]

Finally, there are the trade associations, principally the American Correctional Association:

The hard hat of the ACA is now a great pavilion over a congeries of enterprisers. Proposals, grants and sales are the game. The federal pipe line pours billions of dollars into innumerable jurisdictions, grantees and enjoyers of indirect benefits, the money coming down with a peculiar political and police flavor. State budgets have not been overgenerous with prisons. It must be got from Washington, and getting it has generated a new industry and grant expertise.[30]

The combination of these seemingly disparate processes creates a resistance to change that is larger than the resistance engendered by any one activity. The correctional system is far from a monolith, but opposition to sweeping change— specifically change that threatens the cash flow through the system—can be found among each of its components. The effect is a "drag" on reform—a kind of footdragging that hobbles the slow shuffle of change even further.

What Are the Prospects?

Ultimately, values are at stake. Significant change is unlikely as long as the public, particularly the policy-shaping public, perceives the offender as someone somehow different—and as long as this belief is reinforced by the violence of life around us. But there is more to it than that. As long as we refuse to recognize how integral crime is to our way of life, we will persist in pressing futile reforms. The violence is all ours, not someone else's. We are all guilty of either violent acts or of suborning the violence of others.

This does *not* mean that change is impossible, nor does it mean that nothing should be done. Values can be transformed. Larger processes that influence values will inevitably alter public perceptions of crime and the criminal. And even if a large dose of crime seems unavoidable, we are not without the means to protect ourselves. Until we construct the kind of society where crime is neither the product nor a function of grinding social conditions, those who exploit and harm others, regardless of their motivations, can and must be stopped more effectively. More decisive punishment with proven deterrent effects, coupled with sophisticated crime prevention measures, can and will reduce the most destructive offenses and will, as a result, reduce the overall crime rate.

But excessive optimism is unwarranted and even dangerous. The kinds of changes that society would have to make to bring crime under substantial control would drastically alter the way we organize our lives and the way we choose to govern our society and ourselves. Whether the theory is "alienation," "anomie," "subcultural formation," or "life cycle damage," the brute fact is that crime is deeply embedded in our social structure. We don't really try to curb it; we regulate it—which is to say that we "accept" it and seek only to moderate it. For the airlines industry we have the FAA, and for the railroads the ICC. Similarly, we use the criminal justice system as a means of regulating crime as it flows and ebbs through our social structure.

In this environment, real change is illusory. Too often we see offenders as the enemy, failing to recognize that we are the enemy as well. Those who have what is sought by others have little to gain in a redistribution of those resources, even if they might reduce the disparities that many offenders seek in their small and ineffectual ways to redress. And yet, whatever the causes, we remain savaged by crime. This leaves very little room for honest and durable reform. As long as people prey on others, we must stop them—and with more effective punishments than we have been using—even as we frustratingly seek to ameliorate conditions that are conducive to crime.

Yet I am not that pessimistic. As long as we retain our current values and tolerate the inequities that make real change impossible, it's difficult not to be pessimistic. But along with a growing number of others, I believe that we are at a cultural watershed. We are beginning to see that the tools and institutions we have created to solve our social and economic problems no longer work. This recognition may lead in turn to the recognition that we have the opportunity and the resources to recreate ourselves and, in turn, our institutions. Corrections, and indeed the entire criminal justice process, is a derivative system—it only reflects dominant values. If those values change, our means of dealing with crime will change as well. That is my hope.

Notes

1. Jonathan Casper, *Criminal Justice—the Consumer Perspective*, an NILECJ publication (Washington, D.C.: Government Printing Office, 1972).

2. Ibid., p. 57.

3. Karl Menninger, *The Crime of Punishment* (New York: Viking Press, 1968).

4. Southern Regional Council, "Race Makes a Difference" (Atlanta, Ga., 1969).

5. See *Report of the National Advisory Commission on Civil Disorders* (New York: Bantam, 1968); and National Commission on the Causes and Prevention of Violence, *Staff Report*, vol. 12 (Washington, D.C.: Government Printing Office, 1968).

6. Erik Olin Wright, *The Politics of Punishment* (New York: Harper & Row, 1973), p. 110.

7. David Fogel, *We are the Living Proof* (Cincinnati: The W.H. Anderson Company).

8. Jessica Mitford, *Kind and Usual Punishment* (New York: Knopf, 1973).

9. For a general discussion of the subject, see Stephen Schafer, *The Political Criminal* (New York: Free Press, 1974).

10. Erving Goffman, *Asylums* (New York: Anchor, 1961).

11. See letter to Philip Zimbardo, in "Prisons, Prison Reform, and Prisoners' Rights: California," Hearings before Subcommittee No. 3 of the Committee on the Judiciary, House of Representatives, 92nd Congress, 1st Sess., on Corrections, Part II, October 25, 1971 (Washington, D.C.: Government Printing Office, 1971), p. 110.

12. For a recent report on the Attica riot, see Tom Wicker, *A Time to Die* (New York: Quadrangle, 1975).

13. Fogel, *We are the Living Proof.*

14. Fogel includes a good survey of the new law in his book, but Ronald Goldfarb and Linda Singer are far more comprehensive in their *After Conviction* (New York: Simon and Schuster, 1973).

15. Goldfarb and Singer, *After Conviction.*

16. Charles McKendrick, "Custory and Discipline," in Paul Tappan, ed., *Contemporary Correction* (New York: McGraw-Hill, 1951), p. 160.

17. For a general discussion of the "conservativism" of supervisory personnel, see Donald Cressey, "Sources of Resistance to Innovation in Corrections," in

Offenders as a Correctional Manpower Resource (Joint Commission on Correctional Manpower and Training, Washington, D.C., June 1968).

18. See *Criminal Justice Digest* 3, no. 5 (May 1975):1.

19. Herman Schwartz, in Annual Chief Justice Earl Warren Conference, sponsored by the Roscoe Pound-American Trial Lawyers Foundation, *A Program for Prison Reform*, June 9-10, 1972, p. 50.

20. Joseph Eaton, *Stone Walls Not a Prison Make* (Springfield, Ill.: Charles C. Thomas, 1962).

21. Gene C. Kassebaum, David A. Ward, and Daniel M. Wilner, *Group Treatment by Correctional Personnel*, cited in Wright, *Politics of Punishment*, p. 78.

22. Eaton, *Stone Walls*, p. 134.

23. For a survey of public attitudes, see Eugene Doleschal, "Public Opinion and Correctional Reform," *Crime and Delinquency Literature* 2 (August 1970):465-470; and, more recently, Michael J. Hindelang, "Public Opinion Regarding Crime, Criminal Justice, and Related Topics," *Crime and Delinquency Literature* (December 1974):501-523.

24. Robert Martinson, "What Works?—Questions and Answers About Prison Reform," *The Public Interest* 35 (Spring 1974):22-54; and James O. Robison and Gerald Smith, "The Effectiveness of Correctional Programs," *Crime and Delinquency* 17 (January 1971):67-80.

25. Marvin E. Frankel, *Criminal Sentences* (New York: Hill & Wang, 1973). See also Nigel Walker, *The Aims of the Penal System* (Edinburgh: Edinburgh University Press, 1966), and Willard Gaylin, *Partial Justice* (New York: Harper & Row, 1974).

26. See Andrew Von Hirsch, *The Justice of Punishment*, report of the Committee for the Study of Incarceration (publication pending).

27. See Lawyers' Committee for Civil Rights Under the Law, Sarah Carey, ed., *Law and Disorder* (Committee for Civil Rights Under the Law, 1972).

28. See *Prisoners in State and Federal Institutions on December 31, 1971, 1972, and 1973* (Washington, D.C.: Government Printing Office, 1975); *Survey of Inmates of Local Jails, 1972* (Washington, D.C.: U.S. Department of Justice, n.d.); and *Expenditure and Employment Data for the Criminal Justice System, 1972-73* (Washington, D.C.: Government Printing Office, 1975).

29. See Andrew Rutherford, "The Dissolution of the Training Schools in Massachusetts" (Columbus, Ohio: Academy for Contemporary Problems, 1974); and Lloyd Ohlin, Robert B. Coates and Allen D. Miller, "Radical Correctional Reform: A Case Study of the Massachusetts Youth Correctional System," *Harvard Education Review* 44, no. 1 (1974):74-111.

30. Thomas E. Gaddis, "A Billion-Dollar Industry," *The Nation* (October 22, 1973), p. 403. Reprinted with permission.

Index

Agnew, Spiro, 75
Alschuler, Albert, 92n
American Correctional Association, 118n, 167
American Friends Service Committee, 74-75, 87, 124-125
Ancel, Marc, 26n
Andenaes, Johannes, 29
Ault, Allen, 163

Bailey, William C., 134n
Banfield, Edward, 16-17, 66
Bankston, William, 51n
Beccaria, Cesare, 65
Becker, Gary, 65n
Becker, Howard S., 46
behavioral modification, 35
behavioral science, 42, 48-50
behavioral technology, 32
Bell, Brian, 81n
biological perspective, 42, 43, 47, 59, 61-63
Blumstein, Alfred, 77
Bohlander, Edward W., 118n
Bunker, Edward, 160n

California Treatment Program, 33
Cardozo, Benjamin, 92n
Carey, Sarah, 170n
Casper, Jonathan, 75, 160
Chaiken, Jan M., 70n
change, 145, 159-169 (see also reform and reform movements); pressures for, 85-97
chemotherapy, 63
Chiricos, Theodore, 30
Christie, Nils, 79
Cincinnati National Meeting of 1870, 46n, 49n
Citizens Inquiry on Parole and Criminal Justice of New York, 31, 116n, 117n, 118n
Clark, Ramsey, 31, 46, 49
Cloward, Richard, 44
Coates, Robert, 122n, 170n
Cobb, William, 64, 82n
coercion, 33, 35, 110-112
Cohen, Bernard, 86
Cohen, Jacqueline, 77

Committee for the Study of Incarceration, 26, 61n, 124-125, 131, 151n, 166
Conrad, John, 34n, 138n
contracting, 112-113
Cooper, H.H.A., 53n
corrections, community-based, 11, 24, 34, 37, 98-100, 102-104, 111, 123, 128-130, 133, 135, 143-144, 154, 164; eras of, 8, 23, 36-50; evaluation of, 92-97; policy, 31, 69-73, 141-145; practice, 36, 85-116, 153; theory of, 12, 23-36, 58-72, 85, 121-137
Council on Economic Development, 124-125
Cressey, Donald, 24, 25, 37, 71, 169n
crime, causes of, (see corrections, theory of); constancy, 77-78; definition of, 146; hidden, 48, 78-79; prevention, 27, 66; rates, 15, 17, 18, 30, 57, 59, 67, 142, 166; relativity of, 12, 74-76; victimless, 12, 71, 72, 76-77, 149; violent, 71-73
criminal justice system, 15-19
criminal law, 12, 41, 59, 61, 74-81. See also decriminalization
criminology, 74-81, 150-151; critical, 47, 74-76

dangerousness. See offender, dangerous
decarceration, 97-99, 122, 125, 167
decriminalization, 76-77, 148-149
Delancey Street Foundation, 100n
deterrence, 23, 24, 28-31, 46, 50, 64-66, 78, 94, 127, 130-134, 136, 151-152
deviance, 36-50, 77-80, 146-147
discretion, 15-19, 39, 86, 91-92, 160, 165
diversion, 11, 15, 93, 95-96, 100-102, 150
Doleschal, Eugene, 78-79, 169n
Durkheim, Emile, 44, 47

Eaton, Joseph W., 163
economist's perspective, 31, 64-66, 134, 155

171

About the Author

Rick J. Carlson, a lawyer by training, graduated from the University of Minnesota Law School, practiced law for three years and then served as a research attorney for InterStudy in Minneapolis. He was a visiting fellow at the Center for the Study of Democratic Institutions in Santa Barbara, California, and now lives near San Francisco and works as an itinerant writer and consultant. He is also a Senior Research Associate at the National Academy of Sciences and a Research Associate at the Institute for the Study of Human Knowledge in Palo Alto, California. His other publications include *The End of Medicine* (1975) and *The Frontiers of Science and Medicine* (1975).

Related Lexington Books

Berkson, Larry C., *The Concept of Cruel and Unusual Punishment*, 272 pp., 1975

Dodge, Calvert, *A Nation Without Prisons*, 288 pp., 1975

Smith, Joan, Fried, William, *The Uses of the American Prison*, 192 pp., 1974

Whinery, Leo H., Nagy, Thomas J., Fisher, Kaye D., Sather, Gregory A., *Predictive Sentencing*, In Press